The Fires of Autumn

The Fires of Autumn

Sexual Activity in the Middle and Later Years

by Peter A. Dickinson

DRAKE PUBLISHERS INC.
NEW YORK

Published in 1977 by
Drake Publishers Inc.
801 Second Avenue
New York, N.Y. 10017

Library of Congress Cataloging in Publication Data

Dickinson, Peter, 1927-
    The fires of autumn.

    1. Aged--Sexual behavior.   I. Title.
HQ30.D5   301.41'767   73-18403

ISBN 0-8473-1502-9

Printed in the United States of America

This book is dedicated to those who want to
add *more life to their years* . . .
to those who believe in the *quality of loving*
as well as the *quantity of living.*

CONTENTS

PREFACE

"I may have snow on the roof, but I've still got fire in the furnace!" That vaudeville "oldie" used to raise the roof with hoots, howls, cheers, and leers.

But I wasn't laughing. At the age of fourteen I had "snow on the roof" (white hair) and "fire in the furnace" (a belly full of sex urge). And I didn't think the joke was funny.

Now, several decades later, I've learned that sex is *fun* at any age, but I still don't think it's something to laugh at. On the other hand, although I may take it seriously at times, I don't want to have to read a textbook to find out how to enjoy it more.

Maybe that's why I wrote this book—a warm-hearted treatment of a heartfelt subject. I have other reasons: As Editor-in-Chief of *Harvest Years* (now titled *Retirement Living*) for more than twelve years, I published much helpful information for older readers, including an article entitled "Today's Facts About Senior Sex." In this article I tried to explore the truths and explode the myths about sex in the later years.

The issue was a hit. I received hundreds of requests for extra copies (for that bird-watching article, of course). But I thought I knew the *real* reason, so I reprinted the sex article and advertised it for sale. Within weeks we had requests for more than 100,000 reprints, and it is still selling.

I became a "sexpert"—interviewed on television, radio, over the telephone, and behind the barn. Darned if folks didn't say I knew what I was talking about.

My more serious reason for writing this book is my deep respect for the more technical works in this field, especially the late Dr. Isadore Rubin's *Sexual Life After Sixty*. This excellent book is filled with informative nuggets, but it takes some digging to get out the gold.

Sex is living—not statistics and clinical studies. I've tried to

11

translate factual data into realistic drama—to make the material "live" a little; but in no instance have I distorted facts for sensationalism.

I've tried to appeal to your head as well as your heart, with enough expert advice to be *practical* and enough case histories and interviews to be *personal*.

I've seasoned the book with sugar (romance), spice (sex), salt (humor), and sage (advice). I've added history for perspective, medical facts for authority, personal experience for dramatization, and helpful tips for application. Take that which suits your palate; leave that which doesn't. One way or another, you'll get a hearty meal to nourish both body and soul.

Just as it takes two to tango, it takes more than one to write a book. My heartfelt thanks to Irene Donelson, coauthor of *When You Need a Lawyer* and *Married Today, Single Tomorrow*, for her extensive research and advice; to Irving Ladimer, SJD, Special Counsel/Health Programs, American Arbitration Association, and Kenneth Anderson, former Editor of *Today's Health,* for their material and assistance; to Louise Driggs, Home Economics Consultant, and Walter W. Sackett, Jr., M.D., Representative, Florida State Legislature and Specialist in Gerontology, for their suggestions, and to the following gerontologists, physicians, psychologists, psychiatrists and sociologists who shared their research findings with me: Martin A. Berezin, M.D., Editor of *Journal of Geriatric Psychiatry*; James E. Birren, Ph.D., Director, Ethel Percy Andrus Gerontology Center; Ewald W. Busse, M.D., Chairman of the Department of Psychiatry of Duke University; Mary S. Calderone, M.D., Executive Director, Sex Information and Education Council of the U.S.; Elliott Feigenbaum, M.D., Medical Director, Western Institute of Human Resources; Joseph T. Freeman, M.D., Professor of Medicine in Gerontology, University of Nebraska Medical Center; Herman W. Gruber and Gilbert F. Martin of the American Medical Association; Victor Kassel, M.D., Specialist in Geriatrics; James A. Peterson, Ph.D., Director, Liaison Services, Ethel Percy Andrus Gerontology Center; Eric Pfeiffer, M.D., Professor of Psychiatry, Duke University; Daniel S. Rogers, Information Officer, Gerontology Research Center, the National Institutes of Health; E.J. Scheimann, M.D., Specialist in Geriatric Sexology; and Sondra Gorney, Executive Director of the Information Center on the Mature Woman.

My special thanks to the scores of middle-aged and older men and women who confided in me, so that their experiences might help others to find health and happiness through sexual activity. I've tried to present their experiences objectively and factually. My wife, Brigitte, who as a reference librarian contributed much research for this book, and I are grateful to all of you for making *The Fires of Autumn* a reality.

I
HANG-UPS ARE FOR HYPOCRITES

Why should anyone have sexual hang-ups? If it's because of those prigs, prudes, and pious phonies who gave our ancestors the idea that sex was "evil," let's laugh in their faces.

Among other points, I'm going to prove that most of those "holier-than-thou" types were really swingers in sackcloth, punishing themselves by punishing others. Unfortunately, they sold some people on the idea that sex was sinful.

Frankly, I prefer the "live and let live" attitude of the British actress Mrs. Patrick Campbell, who said some seventy years ago: "I don't care what people do, as long as they don't do it in the streets and frighten the horses." Well, Mrs. Campbell, some people *are* doing it in the streets, and not even the horses are frightened. And the fact that swinging sex has "gone public" doesn't mean it has just been invented.

One might think that sexual taboos are Victorian hangovers that should have evaporated with a more enlightened dawn. But because some taboos do exist, we still must be suffering from the same hang-ups. So let's look at the past to see if sex was any different yesterday than it is today.

The Ancients Had Names for It . . .
The Bible sings the praises of sex, especially in the Song of Songs, in which a lover feels he is climbing a tree as he discovers "in her breasts clusters of the vine and in her breath the odor of apples."

Ancient biblical sages such as King David kept legions of concubines who did housework as well as "homework." And David's son, King Solomon, surpassed all biblical records by having a harem of 300 concubines.

The ancients held that a virgin could rejuvenate an aging man. They knew that King David was gone when they bedded him with a

15

fresh virgin, and he didn't even raise an eyelid.

In Sparta, homosexuality was legislated as part of ordinary life. In those days the lyric poet Pindar could write: "But I, for the goddess's sake, waste away like wax of holy bees under the heat of the sun when I look at the young blooming limbs of boys." And the lesbian Sappho could write to her young bride: "My heart beats, my voice fails, fire runs beneath the skin, the eyes see not, the ears buzz, sweat flows off me, trembling seizes me, and, fading like withered grass, I am as one dead."

In Rome, the ancients used gladiatorial shows to stimulate the sex urge. They were driven mad with excitement as man and beast fought each other to bloody death. Prostitutes took advantage of this lust and intercepted as easy prey those who had just returned from the arena, and brothels opened nearby lest time and distance cool the spectators.

In short, the Romans took sex or lust for granted just as they did death.

I'm not sure that the ancient Chinese advanced sex when they conceived the male and female principles of *yang* and *yin*. According to this concept, men are active, women intuitive; men are interested in things and ideas, women in people and feelings. This idea of sexual separation influenced countless generations, including our own.

Since those times, sexual mythology has had its ups and downs. But it's a myth that marriage existed to legalize sexual enjoyment, and it's a myth that there is little in present-day sexuality that didn't have its parallel in American social history. The younger generation may think times have changed, but what they're doing today was discovered yesterday.

Those Passionate Puritans

The Puritans may have mouthed purity, but they practiced passion. Despite a severe Puritan code, married pilgrims who emigrated to America usually remarried without disclosing earlier ties. One reason was that unmarried men were misfits in the New World; every settler needed a wife as a housekeeper, farm worker, and bearer of young farm workers.

As most of the women died around the age of forty from overwork and overbearing, many men married three or four wives— often without benefit of religious or legal ceremony. In fact, the Brownists, a Puritan sect, ruled that unmarried men and women were free to mate at any time—a fact said to have influenced numerous emigrants to New England.

As one example of religious hypocrisy, let's take the case of a Captain Underhill, who was tried for "having solicited a woman's chastity under the pretense of Christian love." Underhill claimed that he and the good wife were merely praying together to resist temptation. But the evidence was too strong, and he was forced to confess.

To gain forgiveness, Underhill was required to make a detailed public confession of his crime and to fall on his knees before the cuckolded husband. Underhill didn't spare salaciousness or sanctimony: the wronged husband forgave the philanderer and even gave the captain's wife a gift. Thus, Underhill not only had the pleasure (as did the audience) of boasting of his conquest while "confessing," but his deed was condoned by the deceived husband and his own wife.

When we strip away sanctimony, the Puritans were realists who didn't believe in celibacy and who were well aware of the body's hungers. That's why there were always enough "sinners" to appall fainthearted reformers and enrage fanatics. And as Puritan communities grew and prospered, so did their vices.

When that Puritan of Puritans, Cotton Mather, ruled against fornication early in the eighteenth century, he described his own lustful visions in such delectable detail and delivered such lurid descriptions of his temptations that his books and sermons must have stimulated as well as enlightened his audience.

Mather and other religious hypocrites failed, however, to stop their flocks from mingling; church records at Groton, Connecticut, show that of sixteen couples admitted to full communion, nine confessed to fornication before marriage.

Despite severe penalties against bearing illegitimate children, Colonial records reveal such cases. In 1883, Charles Francis Adams, a member of the distinguished Adams family, declared: "The illegitimate child was more commonly met with in the last than in the present century, and bastardy cases furnished a class of business with which country lawyers seem to have been as familiar as they are with liquor cases now."

In Puritan times, fornication was one luxury anyone could afford. Although the act was subject to a fine and hardly a day passed without someone being punished for it, only a few sinners were caught. The persistent lover who entwined his earthly passion with heavenly piousness had a better chance of seduction in Puritan New England than almost anywhere else in the world.

Slavery Made Sex in the South

If religion spurred sex in New England, slavery stimulated sex in the South.

Here again, religion was an excuse. Seventeenth-century Englishmen believed that Africans were descendants of Noah's accursed son Ham and that their black color was a sign of God's disfavor. Thus, slaves were considered little better than animals, and sexual union with them really didn't matter.

Many masters copulated with slaves and fathered their children. Greed combined with lust to make light-colored slaves more marketable. But any slave was a salable commodity, and in some cases black men and women were locked up together until the women became pregnant. In other cases, white men were paid "stud fees" to breed with slaves. Many a slave owner introduced his son to sex by "initiating" him in the slave quarters. The result was that many plantations became "family affairs," with the sons and daughters of slave and master working the fields.

Having debased slave women, the master elevated his own women to pious pedestals. White women became goddesses, surrounded by chivalrous menfolk protecting their ladies fair from revenge-seeking savages.

This must have confused Southern ladies, who knew that their men were seducing the black man's wife and daughter. Some sociologists believe that many white women were secretly torn between fear and desire of black men; maybe they, too, would find more sexual fulfillment with a black lover.

Because of these possible liaisons, white men formed secret societies such as the Ku Klux Klan to mutilate or even murder a black man who was accused—justly or unjustly—of molesting a white woman. In doing so, Klan members sublimated their own guilt and eliminated a sexual rival.

Many Southern white women who knew the truth were disgusted with their men and became sexually unresponsive. So white men turned all the more to sexual pleasure with black women. The products of some of these unions—pretty mulatto girls—became highly prized as prostitutes.

In New Orleans, Creole quadroons and octoroons were trained to become white men's mistresses. To bring master and mistress together, the city held formal quadroon balls where a man might select a girl and bid for her favors. The man—usually married—would then set up his mistress in a love nest, and the association might last for several years.

When the slaves were freed, however, and their economic conditions improved, fewer Negro women were forced, sold, or tempted into prostitution, thus reducing sexual contact between black and white. Nevertheless, despite laws in most Southern states forbidding intermarriage, many white men did continue (and favor) sexual unions with black mistresses.

Was Victoria a Sex Cat?

If rising economic conditions elevated the sexual morals of blacks, it may have lowered those of the whites. The white idle rich and idle poor had the time and/or the money for vice, but to stake out its position a rising middle class looked upon sex with disdain.

This middle class acquired sexual hang-ups during the so-called Victorian era. Victorian morality suppressed easy access to sex and even discussion of it. Women were either "good" or "bad"; love was either "pure" or "evil."

Young men were told to subdue their sexual desires through exercise, cold baths, hard beds, religious exercise, and abstention from French novels. Sex wasn't to be trusted; men and women were always in danger of an "impure" relationship.

These notions probably led to increased homosexuality and masturbation. Some sociologists assert that the Victorians' "war" on masturbation (they said it was a filthy act that could lead to every disorder from bloodshot eyes to lunacy) was motivated by acute guilt.

Religion again added its stimulus. Self-denial became godly; sex became evil. But this emphasis on the "evil" nature of sex only heightened its attractiveness to the lustful male, while the "good" Victorian woman wasn't supposed to be interested. In many instances these notions gave Victorian husbands an excuse for failing to satisfy their wives. "Death before dishonor" became the virtuous slogan; it also drove men to seek sexual satisfaction with prostitutes.

By 1866 Bishop Matthew Simpson of the Methodist Episcopal Church stated that there were more prostitutes than Methodists in New York City. By conservative count, there were 621 houses of prostitution, 75 "concert saloons" of ill repute, and 96 houses of assignation.

The houses of assignation were symbols of Victorian hypocrisy. Situated in the best neighborhoods, they guaranteed privacy to "elegant" ladies and gentlemen (usually lovers married to others).

The man entered by one door, the lady by another. No names were used, and discretion was assured for this form of adultery in the "best" circles.

The irony of all this sexual hypocrisy was that the lady who gave her name to the moralistic age may have been a secret swinger. After Prince Albert's death, Queen Victoria became "intrigued" with a manly Highlander named Brown. Brown was big, brawny, brash, and usually three sheets to the wind. He respected no one—much less the Queen—yet she selected him as her personal footman. Where others stepped softly around Victoria and wouldn't dare intrude upon her privacy, Brown barged in and out of the bedchamber as though he slept there. No one dared rebuke Brown for his familiarities—it was obvious that he was the Queen's favorite.

Stories about their relationship spread through Britain. "Mrs. Brown" jokes circulated, and a favorite tabloid of the day, the *Tomahawk*, kept alive rumors with innuendos and cartoons. One daring cartoon showed a Highlander lolling against a vacant throne, glancing scornfully at a roaring British lion charging up the steps. Other journals picked up the scandal, and one even printed a comic picture showing Brown seated smoking his clay pipe in the Royal Closet with his feet resting on the mantelpiece, while the Queen regarded him happily.

Were Brown and Victoria secret lovers? Most people believe it, and in the Queen's own journal, "Further Leaves from Our Life in the Highlands," she can't stop talking about Brown, detailing what he wore, or ate, or said on a certain day. During Highland dancing, the Queen would dance only with the usually drunk and disrespectful Brown. One letter fragment—believed to be from Victoria to Brown—contained these words: "Forgive me if I offend, but you are so dear to me, so adored, that I cannot bear to live without you."

If this is Victorian morality, why the sexual hang-ups?

Censors and Vicarious Gratification

Censorship whets the appetite, and thus the Victorians were stimulated by suppressed "pornography."

Although most American erotica started as editions of European works, American titles were added depicting "depravity" that today would be considered dull.

Yet a preoccupation with pornography led some men—like Anthony Comstock—to be regarded as pillars of purity.

At the age of thirty, Comstock was so "shocked" at the so-called dirty books of his day that he quit his job at the post office to devote himself to tracking down obscene literature.

He also testified in some scandalous trials and helped to promote strong anti-obscenity bills that became known as the "Comstock Laws." The Post Office Department rewarded him with an appointment as a Special Agent (later Inspector). And for forty years he continued to confiscate "dirty books," including the works of Giovanni Boccaccio, Walt Whitman, and George Bernard Shaw.

Finally, his zeal to suppress sin in art, theater, and sculpture revealed him as a man of little education, taste, or qualifications to judge art or man. Most historians rate him as a frustrated man who satisified his sexual appetites by pursuing smut.

Zealous religious leaders also protested the devil too much. In fact, many religious events and rituals embraced more sexuality than sanctity. Even in sects such as the Shakers—which condemned marriage as gratification of lust—ceremonies were sexual in nature if not in intent. In one ceremony worshippers jumped and shouted as the spirit moved them, and whirled like dervishes. Sessions lasted until early morning hours, when the convulsions and sounds of the participants rivaled the bumps and grinds, moans and groans of the most modern sex orgy.

Other religious sects held beliefs that embraced sexual expression. Among the Mormons, polygamy was adopted after their trek west, first to Missouri and later to Utah. Many Mormon men were killed in the migration, and the practice of polygamy became a social and procreational necessity. For some Mormon men, however, polygamy provided sexual variety and the possibility of finding a woman with special sexual techniques. Polygamy also allowed men to take a succession of younger wives, offering them repeated renewals of desire.

But although polygamy didn't primarily license unorthodox sexual relations, most Americans *thought* it did, and they fed their sexual appetites with what they imagined went on in Mormon "harems." Certainly, the persecution of Mormons stemmed as much from envy as it did from greed and religious repression.

Many other religious groups experimented with communal living. Although communes might be thought of as relatively new, they are actually throwbacks to the past, when they combined humanitarian or religious ideas with a philosophy or theology of sex. The socialist John Humphrey Noyes invented the "complex marriage" at his famous community in Oneida, New York. All men were potential husbands for all women, and children were shared by all adults. The community even had a committee on "marriage pro tem," which would pass on separation if desired.

At one point community life became one continuous courtship, and often young men were initiated by women who were beyond the menopause. In time the system created an "ascending fellowship" in which older members of the community paired off with younger ones.

Camp Meeting Children

Sex and religion fused and flamed at the celebrated camp meetings. These swinging sermons brought release, drama, and hope to the settlers' otherwise dull lives.

Circuit-riding preachers gathered great crowds to some grassy knoll where they orated "hell-fire and brimstone" sermons until their listeners shrieked and wept, writhed and jerked on the ground. They released sexual emotions with "religious ecstasy," and there were always men—including preachers—ready to take advantage of aroused women. So common were births after these sessions that "camp-meeting child" became a common term, and the popular saying was that the camp meetings "made more souls than they saved."

Temperance Tracts That Went Astray

Some of the "Lips that touch liquor shall never touch mine" ladies were even more pious and phony than the preachers. One of the sexiest books I've read was a temperance book written in the 1880's. I bought it as a joke at a secondhand store, but I soon realized that I had a treasure trove of salacious stuff. Although drinkers necessarily met their sordid end, their paths took them through some pretty sexy scenes.

I recall one episode in which a "Big Daddy" Wall Street type was presumably lushing it up in his office when a messenger brought a note that went something like this: "Come and claim your prize before she has a chance to dry her pretty eyes." I suppose at this point "Big Daddy" took another swig before setting off for this fancy place. Going in a secret entrance (did those places *ever* have front doors?), he was ushered into a luxurious room that probably contained a bar as well as a bed.

Sobs and moans rent the air as the fair maid was dragged into the room. But before she could screech "Death before dishonor," she recognized the old goat: "Daddy, thank God, you've come to take me away from this horrible place." That's not what Big Daddy had in mind, but presumedly he preferred intoxication to incest and took another swig as the scene faded . . .

The author mixed every conceivable misadventure with alcohol imbibing, ignoring the fact that alcohol probably inhibits sexual activity rather than stimulates it.

Then there were women who *did* touch a drop. Of course, they became prostitutes or worse, and sunk into alcoholic vapors through luxurious lasciviousness.

Was Freud a Fraud?

We hail the Viennese psychologist Sigmund Freud as a "savior" who liberated the libido. Yet there is evidence that Freud was a sexual anemic who tried to invigorate his own sexual life.

At the age of forty-one Freud wrote to his friend Wilhelm Fliess: "Sexual excitation is of no more use to a person like me." On one occasion while in his forties, Freud felt physically attracted to a young woman and half voluntarily touched her slightly. He commented on how surprised he was to find that it was still possible for him to feel such attraction.

Yet Freud's writing profoundly influenced American morals. His ideas on freeing sexual instincts and the dangers of sublimation were considered so radical that they were scarcely mentioned in print (Webster's Dictionary did not include the word—or definition—of *Freudian* until 1927), but they were discussed in intellectual circles. They metamorphosed some women, who blamed sexual repression for everything from vomiting to obsessions. And Freud's observations that forms of sublimation included irrational devotion to the church, the army, and the state challenged some of our noblest institutions.

These theories—coupled with improved means of birth control —ushered in the 1900's with their double entendres, "yellow journalism," and "ragtime" (actually ragged-time music). New dance steps swept the country: the Turkey Trot, Grizzly Bear, Kangaroo Dip, and Bunny Hug. Both music and steps suggested if not simulated sex; even the Vatican recognized the implications and issued a decree: "The music must stop!" Like many religious edicts, it served merely to publicize the vice and helped pay the piper.

Then came the disillusionments of World War I and the "loose morals" of the "Roaring Twenties." Boys were "sheiks," girls were "flappers" (a word borrowed from nineteenth-century English slang meaning "unruly girl"). The flapper's short skirt revealed stockings rolled above or below the knee, her short hair was marcelled or curled, and her mouth was made up into a Cupid's bow. In *Only Yesterday*, Frederick Lewis Allen described the flappers as "men's casual and light-hearted companions; not broad-hipped mothers of the race, but irresponsible playmates."

It is questionable just how much more irresponsible flappers were than their mothers. Petting was popular, and the "sheik's" flask and rumble-seated car must have led more than one couple "down the primrose path." Indeed, many moralists thought that "flaming youth" was at the steering wheel of the family car hell-bent for some sinful place. And their hangovers led to the Great Depression.

The 1930's did sober the nation and tame its morals. In 1936 *Fortune* surveyed college youth and concluded that "sex is no longer news." Both sexes sought security, rather than adventure or radical behavior. Although more people had more time on their hands, they lived their dreams through soap operas and lavish motion pictures.

World War II contributed its own moral climate. "Dear John" letters told many a soldier that his wife no longer cared, and many a soldier had a "surrogate wife" overseas. Conquering heroes confiscated the morals of the losers, with resulting occupation offspring.

But if World War II brought more realistic sex behavior, it didn't help the older generation. When young undergraduates at Brandeis University were asked (in the late 1950's) to complete the sentence, "Sex for most old people . . . " almost half the students (ranging in age from seventeen to twenty-three) answered "negligible," "unimportant," or "past."

Has There Really Been a Sexual Revolution?

If we're really having a sexual revolution, it is because of past events, not present morality. Birth control, abortion, sex stimulants are all products of ancient cultures. Even today's sensual water beds are products of bygone hydrotherapists (water doctors) who regularly prescribed cold wet sheets, baths, and douches.

Those who feel we've just begun to "tell it like it is" would have rallied to the banner of the anarchist publication *The Word*, which advocated "free land, free labor, and free love." Persons who currently think of Boston as the seat of purity would be interested in knowing that it was the meeting place (in 1876) of the Sexual Science Association.

In short, the sexual-revolution myth still persists and still influences the way people act. But two researchers, Professors John H. Gagnon and William Simon, who formerly worked at the Institute of Sex Research in Bloomington, Indiana claim that today's sexual patterns are more conservative than those of the past.

If there was a real change, it probably developed around the early part of this century, and its effects continue. In these last decades, the woman has been liberated in both sexual activity and from fear of pregnancy.

Whatever sexual revolution the young may think they're in is really a longing to get *back* to what they feel is a more natural life where intimate relations are openly formed. Thus, communal living, folk music and primitive rhythms, unorthodox clothing and ways of life are all part of a yearning for what the young feel was a simpler and more honest past.

If people believe, however, that they are in the midst of a sexual revolution, they will act as if it were true. This builds pressure, pushing many people to defy their instincts, their heritage, and even their common sense.

In his book *The New Sexuality*, Father Eugene C. Kennedy writes: "The sexual revolution has happened and it has not happened. It has happened because people want to believe that it has, and it has not happened because the evidence doesn't suggest widespread changes in sexual behavior." He adds: " . . . What we need is an authentic rediscovery of sex in the context of human personality . . . a first step in the right direction would be the destruction of the idea that there is anything really new or surprising in the supposed sexual revolution of the day."

What About Older People?

The older we are, the more we should realize what is and what isn't "revolutionary" in sexual relations. However, one advantage we can take from any supposed revolution is that we can use the social climate to expand our own sexual horizons.

Dr. Ewald W. Busse, chairman of the Department of Psychiatry at Duke University, said in a recent speech: "It would appear that sex activity in older persons is gradually responding to changes in our social environment . . . I believe that as the middle-aged and younger people move into the older generation, we are going to see even more remarkable shifts in sexual attitudes in the older age groups."

Perhaps those in their forties or fifties are more likely to be in the midst of a sexual revolution. They've seen the institutions that put the lid on their libidos—the church, schools, government—challenged by the young. They have seen the development of the morning-after pill and the advent of co-ed dormitories.

They've seen yesterday's amateurish black-and-white, silent stag films blossom into today's professional four-color, hard-core pornography, and "just plain sex" surplanted by . . . you name it.

Today's books and pictures are raw and unretouched; "live acts" simulate or stimulate the "real thing." Mechanical devices have replaced normal genitals. The book *The Sensuous Woman* offers a formula for ecstasy featuring a mechanical dildo instead of a phallus, and one sexual study even recommends a vibrator for masturbation as the ultimate in female sexual pleasure.

Women's Liberation gives new status to lesbianism; bisexuality may be the "coming thing" if unisex takes hold.

Newspapers advertise for couples or assorted singles for swapping and other sex games, and divorces become more common among those married fifteen years or longer. Divorces are usually preceded by infidelity by one spouse or both. A Kinsey report several years ago showed that by the age of forty about 50 percent of all husbands and about 25 percent of all wives have engaged in extramarital relations, and these percentages are rising.

On the other side of the mattress, however, are those people who take on the slow, ponderous, fixed habits of age before it's necessary. The men and women who act "old" in their sexual activity before their bodies have really called a halt become sexually old before their time.

Doctors point out that persons who abandon their sexual life early are generally those who are handicapped by neurotic conflicts that involve their sexual emotions, and unconsciously welcome age to abandon a function that has frightened them since childhood.

When people lose their sense of identity, they often choose one of the stereotypes that society casts for them. These stereotypes include the "sexlessness" of old age. Of all the myths that surround sexuality in our culture, perhaps none is so widespread as the belief that older people are no longer interested in sex and are unable to engage in sexual activities.

What Are Our Sexual Needs As We Grow Older?

"Older people have the same emotional and sexual needs as younger people, with equivalent variations in intensity, kinds of expression, other persons to express with," says Mary S. Calderone,

M.D., Executive Director of Sex Information and Education Council of the U.S. (SIECUS). "As human beings at any stage of life, we long for other human beings to respond to us and to be responsive with—whether in touch, in shared pleasures, joys, sorrows, intellectual interchange, or from time to time in sexual responsiveness at many levels including the purely physical."

She adds that these needs include touching, kissing, embracing. "At this stage of life, who is competent to assume the authority to draw the fine, sensitive line in deciding for others what is moral or immoral, or whether a door must remain open despite a longing for the privacy that those in control take for granted themselves," says Dr. Calderone.

"No age is an automatic cut-off for sex," wrote the late Dr. Isadore Rubin in his book *Sexual Life After Sixty*. But, he continued: "Sexuality cannot flourish in a climate where rejection of aging as a worthwhile stage of life leads inevitably to self-rejection by many older persons . . . "

In some cases it seems that what is "virility" at age twenty-five becomes "lechery" at age sixty-five. Older men are frequently ridiculed as impotent or as "dirty old men." Women are said to be sexually "over the hill" at age fifty.

Sex, self-esteem, and self-image are closely related. If "the spirit is willing but the flesh is weak," it may be more of a case of mind over matter. Perhaps marital or sex counseling might help. And perhaps just a few ideas—like the fact that sex may be easier and more enjoyable when you're fresh in the morning rather than tired at night.

You've Got It—And You'll Always Have It

"Human beings are born with libido and they die with it," says Dr. Stanley R. Dean, clinical professor of psychiatry at the University of Florida College of Medicine. And he asserts that although a person of sixty may not be the sexual acrobat he was at thirty, "he can still walk even though he might not be able to run."

Dr. Dean suggests that a person may have to settle for a less strenuous role than he did before, and that this might lead to such practices as oral-genital sex and other types of uninhibited erotic behavior.

Dr. Dean adds that although some would regard such sexual activities as "depraved" and the participants as "dirty," one elderly patient protested: "I'm not a dirty old man, I'm just a sexy senior citizen!"

Not surprisingly, the doctor says that "checkers, shuffleboard, and pinochle are by no means their only passions." He cited recent news items:

- A prostitute was arrested for soliciting two vice-squad detectives. Her age: sixty-three.
- A frantic husband whose wife had run off with a new love hunted her down, shot her, and then shot himself. Both husband (seventy-five) and wife (seventy) survived.
- A frustrated lothario hurled a makeshift Molotov cocktail consisting of a prune-juice bottle filled with kerosene through the window of his unfaithful lady. His age: seventy-eight.
- A jealous husband caught his wife in bed with another man and blasted him with a shotgun. The unfaithful wife was sixty-five, the husband eighty-one.

And then there's the Sun City, Florida, former model of eighty-two who boasts that she and her man of seventy-two " . . . dance, ride bicycles, go out to dinner . . . do everything—just everything!"

You can do just everything—if you really want to do it. Getting rid of any sexual hang-ups is the first step, and that's just a case of mind over matter.

II
SEXUAL LURES AND ALLURES

In seeking the fountain of youth, Juan Ponce de Léon discovered Florida. In discovering Florida, some people seek their Fountain of Youth. On a recent trip to Miami Beach, I visited a lawyer friend, a man in his sixties who had recently married a woman in her forties.

After a couple of predinner cocktails, and a discussion of this book, my friend confided that he " . . . had sex the night before, sex this morning, and probably would have sex this evening." When I asked him his secret, he replied solemnly: "Massive doses of hormones, Vitamin E, and pornography."

I don't know if he was kidding, but before the evening was ended his wife had fallen asleep, I was exhausted, and he was still cavorting about.

Again mind over matter? Whatever the reason, men through the centuries have sought the "Fountain of Youth." We may laugh at the ancients who ate tiger testicles, inhaled the breath of young girls, and quaffed various love potions—but we're still in the century of monkey-gland transplants, royal jelly, sex foods and pills, and cell therapy. Sex merchants encourage women to buy skin youthifiers, wrinkle removers, bust builders, and hormone filled cosmetics. Hucksters bombard men with potency pills, sex stimulators, and mechanical devices.

Basically these "sex rejuvenators" fall into four categories: (1) edibles and elixirs (drugs in liquid form with an alcohol base); (2) exercises; (3) adornments; and (4) gadgets. I can't endorse any of these aphrodisiacs. In fact, some of them are not only ineffective but dangerous as well! There is, however, a great deal of interest in the subject, so let's examine some of these sexual lures and allures to see how they originated, how they are supposed to work, and how beneficial they actually are.

Things to Eat and Drink (Edibles and Elixirs)

Aphrodisiacs (named after Aphrodite, the Greek goddess of love) are drugs and foods supposedly capable of increasing sexual desire or response in men and women in three ways: (a) reducing fears and inhibitions; (b) enhancing sensitivity; and (c) increasing sexual strength and vigor.

Many ancient aphrodisiacs literally stank; they were concocted of asses' milk mixed with bats' blood, frogs' bones, cow dung, and human excrement. Some aphrodisiacs resembled genital organs in shape (eryngo roots, asparagus), and many herbs and spices were credited with arousing sexual powers by irritating the lining of the genital or urinary tract or by flushing the skin.

The names of some aphrodisiacs enriched our language. The biblical name Issacher stems from the word "sachar" (meaning to hire for wages). It seems that Rachel, the wife of Jacob, was barren and desired the mandrake root (which not only stank but looked like a standing man with an erection) to make her fertile. Leah had the root, and Rachel traded her husband for it. The root failed to work for Rachel, but a night with Jacob made Leah pregnant, and the result was her son, Issacher.

The Romans believed that seed begot seed; they put semen in their aphrodisiacs. The Greeks thought beans (which looked like testicles) were sexy, and the sexiest ancients, the Venetians, were so obsessed with love potions that the rulers outlawed them.

Love potions gave rise to certain superstitions. To the Hebrews, salt symbolized semen; spilling it (salt or semen) on the ground was considered bad luck.

Although none of these sex foods or drinks were scientifically valid, they had this in common: they *seemed* to work if the person using them *thought* they might work (a reverse twist to mind over matter).

New Shakes to Old Love Potions

Many present-day tonics and sex foods are updated versions of older aphrodisiacs. The "Nuxated Iron" of Civil War days was updated into the He-Man Tonic advertised by heavyweight champions Jess Willard and Jack Dempsey (Dempsey took over the testimonial when he whipped Willard—who perhaps had forgotten to take his tonic that morning).

"Princess Lotus Blossom" (née Violet McNeal) claimed to possess the "secret of the Chinese Emperor's virility" (rumored to be the powdered organs of a male turtle) and peddled it as "Vital Sparks." Authorities later found that she made the "sparks" by dumping buckshot candy into a bureau drawer, dampening it, and rolling it around in powdered aloes (a bitter-tasting plant with laxative and tonic qualities).

Many "elixirs," tonics, potions, and "waters" owed their popularity to a liberal content of alcohol. Lydia Pinkham's vegetable compound was laced with 18 percent alcohol, and many present-day tonics also contain an alcoholic "kicker." Many other products contained caffeine, perhaps equivalent to two or three cups of coffee. Under other names (and at much lower prices) they were sold simply to prevent dozing.

Wines, brandy (that alcoholic kicker), "secret herbs," and condensed milk make a powerful aphrodisiac for Bahama islanders. The Haitians drink a brew made of the pega pelo vine; the Russians mix ground antlers with alcoholic brine; and many natives take to powdered rhinoceros horn sprinkled into a drink.

According to the *Encyclopaedia Britannica,* however: "With the exception of alcoholic drinks and certain narcotics, such as marijuana, which may lead to sexual excitation through depression of inhibitory centers, modern medical science recognizes a very limited number of aphrodisiacs. These are, principally, cantharides and yohimbine."

Yohimbine, made from the bark of a Central African tree, may stimulate sexual desire—if taken in poisonous amounts. Cantharides (crushed, dried bodies of beetles—also called "Spanish fly") when swallowed can cause vomiting, bloody diarrhea, urinary irritation, and even death.

The *Encyclopaedia* adds: The reputation of various exotic foods, in particular certain fish, vegetables, and spices, rests not on fact but folklore."

But in spite of current advertising and labeling regulations, hucksters peddle many questionable products. Usually the operators are savvy enough (often through prior convictions) to promote their products by indirect association, implied benefits, and the power of suggestion. The products may "work" (the power of suggestion) for a while, but fears and worries usually return, and the problem remains.

Doctors say that regular foods are better "aphrodisiacs" than oysters, special rye bread, passion fruit, and alcohol. Certain addictive and narcotic drugs (including alcohol) repress sexual activity rather than stimulate it. As Shakespeare said about alcohol:

" ... too much provokes the desire, but it takes away the perfor-mance."

The American Medical Association states: "There is no drug or nutrient generally available for all persons which can increase desire or provide virility in otherwise healthy people. Sexual activity con-tinues until late in life for many people, but there is no self-medication that can insure this."

Pill-popping for Potency

Along with special foods and drinks, many people take various pills to pep up potency. Take the "Golden 50 Tablets" and its promotional material, "Facts for Folks Over 50!" which suggested, among other things, that they were "effective for loss of enjoyment of life ... inability to be the man and woman formerly possible." The U.S. Food and Drug Administration took a dim view of that statement, and the product has vanished from the market.

Unfortunately, many sex-pill peddlers claim that their vitamin-containing products combat "lack of pep, energy, and sexual vigor." These deficiencies may be caused by many ailments, the least of which might be vitamin deficiency. Dr. Victor Herbert, of the Har-vard Medical School, said: "When all the cases of vitamin deficiency reported in the United States in a single year are added up, they don't reach 20,000."

If you eat a normal diet, you'll get all the vitamins and minerals you need. If you eat a poor diet, vitamin and mineral supplements won't help much. And whatever your source of vitamins and min-erals, your body promptly eliminates excesses of Vitamin C and the B complex and stores excesses of Vitamins A and D in the liver and other organs.

If you eat leafy green vegetables, whole-grain breads and cereals, nuts, and organ meats, you should get plenty of Vitamin E—the nutrient billed as "essential for virility" ... "best known for its direct beneficial effect on the sex organs." Hucksters have also touted Vigamin E as a hair restorer and as a prevention or cure for ulcers, skin disorders, lung diseases—and aging.

According to the Food and Drug Administration (F.D.A.), the chief function of Vitamin E is as an antioxidant (that is, it prevents substances from combining with oxygen, thus acting as a preserva-tive, because oxygen speeds utilization). Although certain forms of food processing may destroy some Vitamin E, consumption of a variety of common foods should give you an ample supply of this and other vitamins. Generally, added vitamins won't provide zest or zip where it didn't exist before.

The National Academy of Sciences reports, "There is no clinical evidence that Vitamin E will cure cancer or heart disease." And the F.D.A. adds: " . . . Vitamin E has not been proven to have any of the 'miraculous' effects being claimed for it. We see no reason for a person in good health and eating a well-balanced diet to use a dietary supplement."

Before the F.D.A. clamped down, advocates of "royal jelly" (a milky-looking substance making up the special food of the queen honey bee) pointed to the queen's amazing sexual prowess (she can produce as many as 2,500 eggs—twice her weight) and claimed that what the queen bee ate could " . . . buy you the secret for which man has sought ever since the days when Ponce de Léon searched in vain for the legendary Fountain of Youth."

More specifically, royal jelly was supposed to "restore sex virility in men"; "restore youthful sex functions in women experiencing the change of life and make them fertile again"; "cure all the ills of old age and lengthen the life span." Thus, promoters used royal jelly as an ingredient in sex foods, elixirs, and cosmetics.

But according to scientists, the main components of royal jelly are two B-group vitamins readily available in a normal diet. And the F.D.A. stated: " . . . we have not seen any convincing evidence that royal jelly has any value whatever when used by man either as a food, a drug, or as a cosmetic."

Things to Do (Exercises and Adornments)

There are many things you can *do* to stimulate sexuality. Most obvious is the *kiss*, which titillates the senses of taste, touch, smell, and sound. Even the Eskimo kiss (rubbing noses) titillates these senses. Kisses come in infinite varieties: from Rodin's complete entwinement of body and soul to the reassuring "peck" that reminds one that you still care.

The mucous membranes and complex nervous system of the mouth make it ideal for love (smoking may be a substitute for this pleasure, but kissing is healthier).

The mouth also supplies the life force—breath. The ancient Chinese used breathing exercises to improve sexual activity by forcing air into body recesses, in hopes of vitalizing the sexual fluid.

The sense of smell goes with breathing and kissing. Nearly all animals (including humans) emit odors that announce sexual excitement. It happens with insects; if the female bobyx butterfly is placed in a closed box, males still flock around even thought they can't see her. In fact, man destroys insects by devising synthetic sex odors that lure the insects into traps.

Creams and Salves for Every Occasion

To accent sexual odors, humans through the centuries have used scented salves and perfumes. Cleopatra used "sexual" ointments to ensnare Caesar and then Anthony, and today's sexy advertisements proclaim: "People like you *very much* when you smell nice. Perfume lets you smell right for any (and every) kind of lover . . . "

Besides perfume, entrepreneurs have introduced other exotic ingredients into creams and salves. A Slavic doctor became the toast of Broadway when he presented "Bulgarian rose petal facials." Polly Bergen scored a hit when she introduced a turtle-oil line of cosmetics (the turtle is a symbol of longevity). Other entrepreneurs made fortunes by infusing their creams with hormones, estrogen, animal-gland extracts, carbons, oils, paints, greases, acids, alcohol, lanolin, dyes, borax, lectin, seaweed, and you name it.

Salves and lotions are not confined to cosmetics. The "bosom builders" use common cold creams—occasionally containing an agent that reddens the skin—which depend upon massage and surface circulation. The breast has no muscle, however, and no amount of exercise will do any good except that which (like swimming) streng-thens the pectoral chest muscles and may lift the breasts, thus giving an appearance of breast development.

The products marketed as "stay" or "delay" creams that "magically postpone ejaculation" are essentially some form of benzo-caine—a surface analgesic or pain reliever often used to soothe cuts, burns, and bruises. Sold as a "stay cream" the product may sell for $30; sold to soothe cuts, burns, and bruises it may cost only 90¢.

Exercises for Sexual Stimulation

An older woman, a vegetarian who practices yoga, says: "To you younger sisters, vegetables and headstands may not seem to be the pot of gold at the end of the rainbow, but if you haven't tried it, don't knock it!"

People have used various exercises, apparatus, and gadgets for centuries to stimulate and perfect sexual enjoyment. Sexual exercise tones you up better than jogging—and it's probably healthier for you. These exercises include the training and use of the vaginal and pelvic muscles.

Some people try to "recharge their batteries" through various apparatus. In the California desert, George W. Van Tassel installed an "Integratron," a 38-by-54-foot dome equipped with armatures, air compressors, and turbines to produce up to 100,000,000 volts. Prospective rejuvenates are supposed to walk in a 270-degree arc under the armatures to literally "recharge their batteries." Another device is the "orgone box," a zinc-lined pine box in which a rejuvenate sits to absorb "orgone energy."

Not surprisingly, the bed became a sexual apparatus. In London, in the last century, a Dr. James Graham invented the "Celestial Bed," a great electro-magnetic structure measuring 12 by 9 feet and supported by forty pillars of brilliant glass. The mattress was filled with rose leaves, lavender, and oriental spices; the glass pillars gave off musical sounds. The magnets were supposed to cure impotency and sterility by "pouring forth their magnetic tide." To be on the safe side (and add a little show biz), Graham hired a group of attractive women to perform erotic dances around the bed . . . some nudes even hopped into bed. One of these dancers was Emma Lyon, who later became Lady Hamilton.

Although hydrotherapy isn't new (see Chapter I), water beds are enjoying a current popularity. You "move with the current" in a water bed and set up a natural rhythm, which takes over. Many couples try it for a "second honeymoon," registering at a motel or hotel featuring these inflated sex mattresses.

Sex Dictates the Fashions

Sex has dictated many styles and types of clothing. In most cases garments were designed not to cover but to reveal or emphasize certain parts of the body.

Garments also camouflaged certain sexual mishaps. History says that a famous concubine of an eighth-century Chinese emperor invented the brassiere. While having an affair with one of the emperor's generals, in a moment of passion the illicit lover bit one of her breasts, leaving marks. She was scheduled to visit the emperor that night; how could she hide the passion mark?

She did so by teasingly draping a red silk apron around her bosom. The emperor liked the new "game" so much that the idea spread throughout the court, and other ladies adopted bras, even padding and embroidering them.

Men also adopted sexual garments, though originally for a

different reason. To safeguard his genitals, the ancient warrior securely sheathed them. As fashion and warfare became more refined, he decorated and embroidered this sheath. In peacetime, he transformed this sheath into a "sex glove"—an outside pocket to hold and even emphasize his genitals. Going even further, some men padded or stuffed this pocket in front to hold money or pieces of fruit to lure susceptible ladies.

Certain charms became sexual fashion. Pliny the Elder tells of an aphrodisiac bracelet containing the right testis of an ass—regarded as a particularly lascivious animal.

The fig tree, leaves, and plants were—and are—sex symbols. The prolific tree became a symbol of fertility, the leaves (thanks to Adam and Eve) a symbol of modesty, and the fruit (with its likeness to the male genitals) a sexual good luck charm. Even today, many of the best educated and most cultured people in Italy, Spain, and Portugal wear a good-luck charm called a *figa*, consisting of a fist, symbolizing the vulva, with the thumb (held between the first two fingers) signifying the penis. In Mexico, the natives attach the *figa* to church walls as offerings of thanks.

The fig tree was sacred to the Greek god Priapus, worshiped as the promoter of procreation and often depicted with an enormous erect penis.

The phallus charm, made of clay, wood, silver, gold, or glass, became a symbol of all life. It was displayed as a sign, a necklace, and a good luck charm. Bakers and confectioners made phallus-shaped products that their patrons ate for good luck and virility. And the phallus was the magic wand that protected people against frigidity, sterility, and attack.

Things to Use (Gadgets and Apparatus)

Some phalluses aren't so lucky. Whereas size of the penis has little to do with sexual effectiveness, it must be erect to perform.

Thus, a number of sex merchants devised splints, suction devices, rings, and dildoes to extend, support, strengthen (or take the place of) the male organ.

Unfortunately, some devices are downright dangerous as well as disgusting. A hard extension may physically and emotionally turn off a female. The penis ring, which cuts off the flow of blood to sustain an erection, may work for a while, but if not fitted by a physician, it can also cause undue engorgement and soreness.

Sex merchants have also devised numerous devices to stimulate women. Basically, these devices consist of a soft rubber or plastic ring that fits over the penis, with dorsal extensions on which are molded several soft studs or spines. With each coital thrust, the soft studs rub to and fro across the clitoris, producing stimulation.

Other dubious devices include the suction breast developers and the electrode anal-shock thrill devices. Although many gadgets aren't outright frauds, medical and technical scientists disagree as to their safety and effectiveness. Many rosy claims are considered puffery, but they can't be labeled as completely false or misleading.

Manufacturers and promoters of these shady products usually have an alternate line of services or products to replace any that are confiscated, and some operate on the "parking lot" principle, expecting to be caught and considering the resulting fine as part of the cost of doing business, then proceeding as before under another name.

Sexual Toys as Outlets

Some people use sexual toys, alone or with a partner, to bring about orgasm. In describing these devices, I am focusing on reality; they are used for various reasons—some therapeutic. Although I am not recommending anything, I am pointing out that these mechanical substitutes can have their proper place in a person's sexual outlets.

Throughout the centuries, men have used some form of vaginal substitute. Forms available today include inflatable, full-size "party dolls" (some with rudimentary clefts between the legs). Other vaginal substitutes consist of foam-rubber or warm-water containers with plastic or rubber vaginas. The difficulty with most such devices is that the opening does not stretch and is not "form-fitted" for every man.

The same might be said of the dildo, or artificial penis, used by women. Also, vaginal penetration isn't as important to a woman as clitoral stimulation. The female usually has an orgasm because thrusts of the penis pull the clitoris back and forth over the pubic bone, rubbing it rhythmically between the folds or upper edges of the outer vaginal lips. The dildo does not provide the warmth and overall physical contact of regular intercourse.

However, these devices may "turn on" a partner who watches them used, and they may signal what the partners can do in practice.

Women have long used the exotic and effective Japanese *rin-no-tama*. It consists of two hollow metal balls, one empty and the other containing a smaller ball, lead pellets, or mercury. The woman puts the empty ball into the vagina first, then the filled one. A tampon keeps them in place. From then on, any movement—including walking—makes the balls bounce, causing sensations within the vagina.

Vibrators are modern, safe, and sensuous instruments that have their place in physical as well as sexual therapy. Women who are reluctant to masturbate by hand may psychologically accept the impersonal stimulation of a vibrator.

Penis shaped vibrators can be used to apply relaxing (or stimulating) massage to any part of the qody; they are powered by a battery that energizes a pulsating tip. Such vibrators can be bought at many drugstores or novelty shops, or by mail order. They cost from $3 to $20 depending upon size; the standard size is about 7 inches long.

The main value of the vibrator lies in the fact that it may be a psychologically acceptable impersonal guide to a woman's erogenous zones, helping her to discover herself and offering her a needed outlet when other means aren't available. However, one widow said:

"I became extremely nervous after George died; I was smart enough to recognize that I needed a sexual outlet. I masturbated when in my early teens, but I gave it up as 'naughty.' It would have been hard to start masturbating after all these years, and it would have been harder to find a sexual partner my age.

"I had read about vibrators, heard they were safe and acceptable, and knew I could buy one easily at the drugstore. So I did and tried it that night when I was alone.

"Well—the sensation was unbelievable. When I passed the vibrator over my nipples and vulva, I had a tremendous orgasm. But then I felt lonely. There wasn't anyone to talk to, to share the experience.

"I have nothing against it . . . I can see how the vibrator can help me when nothing else is available. I even think in time it can teach me not to be ashamed to masturbate myself. Even if it's my own fingers stimulating me, I want a personal touch."

General Vibrators for Therapeutic Use

Most drugstores also sell the general or "Swedish" vibrator used by barbers, masseurs, physical therapists, and doctors. It costs about $30, operates from an extension cord, and has a 4-by-2-inch superstructure that houses a two- or three-speed electric motor. You strap this vibrator to the back of your hand, and it turns your palm and fingers into pulsators. You can even buy rubber heads to direct stimulation where you want it, when you want it.

General vibrators are great for easing sore muscles and for relaxing a tired body. They also can provide a good sexual "warm-up." If one partner feels tired, the other can run the vibrator over muscles and up and down the spine until the weary one feels relaxed, refreshed, and ready for sex.

As the general vibrator allows the "operator" to stimulate the partner without exerting himself, the operator has a grandstand seat to watch pleasure and excitement mount in the partner. Doctors have recognized the therapeutic and soothing aspects of vibrators for years; these same doctors are now recognizing that they may play an important role in providing valid outlets for people who have no other means of sexual expression, for partners who need or want a helping hand in warming up and enjoying sex in the middle and later years.

The Evergreen Adventure of Sex

We grow old the minute we stop exploring—with our bodies as well as our minds. Like many things we do, we can get in a rut with our sex lives.

Sex celebrates living; lose interest in sex and we lose interest in living.

Whether or not you approve of some modern approaches, be frank with yourself and your sexual partner. If sex has lost its sparkle, maybe it's the routine that's dull, not the desire. And what you probably need is a psychological lift, rather than a mechanical one.

Perhaps a physical examination and an open discussion with your family doctor might help. Just knowing more about our general physical condition can do much to gain ascendency of mind over matter.

A doctor told me of a man in his sixties, with a wife in her fifties, who had to frequent prostitutes because his wife felt they were too old for sex. The man disliked what he did, but he couldn't deny his sex urges. Finally he went to the doctor and blurted out:

"If I could convince myself that sex is sex no matter how old you are, I'd feel a lot better about myself, my wife, and what I'm doing. But I can't seem to get serious, helpful, thoughtful advice from anybody. I may be gray-haired and stooped, but I haven't lost my love for life. I love my wife and I want to make love to her. But she says we're too old for those 'antics.' What am I supposed to do? Sneak sex like a child sneaks cookies from a kitchen jar?"

Unfortunately, the wife had adopted society's attitude that frowns upon grandparents cavorting in bed. This attitude was emphasized recently by a nurse who told me that in her medical ward they didn't take sexual history after age fifty. And she added: "Elderly people can't express their sexual needs because society says that after a certain age they shouldn't be interested in sex. If they do talk about sexual needs, someone is going to call them crazy—and the first ones are themselves."

It seems that we all need sex education—the young, the old, the layman, and the physician. Society has to learn that sexual needs and desires last as long as living—that sex is a celebration of living.

We can all learn new enjoyment at any age. Fortunately, we have sources of helpful information and valid aids for the mind and body, which we shall explore in the next chapter.

We won't have to seek the Fountain of Youth like Ponce de Léon, because we know that the secret of sexual rejuvenation lies in the wellspring of our minds. And we won't have to adopt the " . . . hormone, Vitamin E, and pornography" formula of my lawyer friend because we can take comfort in another scientific report by researchers for the late Dr. Alfred Kinsey:

"Good health, sufficient exercise, and plenty of sleep still remain the most effective aphrodisiacs known to man . . . "

III
HOW TO KEEP IT ROLLING

"When I talk about sex to my children, they snicker. When I talk about sex to my friends, they laugh. Isn't there someone I can talk to . . . some place to get good advice?"

This senior's remarks and the comments of many others convinced me that society's attitude isn't fully receptive to discussion of sex in the later years.

Dr. Eric Pfeiffer, professor of psychiatry, Duke University, says: "A very negative stereotype exists about sex in old people. It says that older people no longer have any sexual interest or feelings, or that they no longer should have them, or if they say they do they are lying or bragging, or they are perverted, dirty old men and women. Such prejudices exist not only in society generally but among the aged themselves . . . they exist also and very strongly so among members of the health and social services professions."

Perhaps one reason is that many people still think sex is intended only for procreation, not recreation. But nature continues producing sex hormones in both men and women long after reproduction is considered unfeasible. These hormones stimulate the whole system, especially the brain and nervous system.

The Adult's Version of the Birds and the Bees
A woman in a senior center asked me, "Why, if there are all those sex education classes for children, isn't there sex education for our age group?" She was just one of many widows I interviewed who hesitated to remarry or engage in active sex because they equated sex with youth.

This woman and others were longing to get good advice. In fact, in analyzing questions that older patients ask their doctors, men seek information on impotence, premature ejaculation, genital size, homosexuality, and masturbation, and women want to know about fertility and sterility, orgasm, vaginal care, and breast problems.

Where can they get this information? Their family doctor may be too busy to ask (or answer) the right questions, or too inhibited or uninformed to discuss these problems. Whereas doctors may know how the body works, they may not know how to make it respond to sexual desires—as we'll discuss later on. This leaves the sex merchants and hucksters all too willing to fill the void.

Unanswered sexual questions and anxieties can speed us into premature aging and loss of potency (ability to have sexual inter-course). I remember the man who became alarmed when he noticed that it took him longer and longer to get an erection. The longer it took, the more worried he became. Finally he consulted a doctor, who told him that his condition was a "natural" accompaniment of growing older—that he was losing his potency. The "advice" only deepened the man's anxiety.

Those of us in good health who are mentally alert should be able to enjoy active sex well into our eighties. Just by learning what you can expect and how to cope can help you continue functioning longer. For instance, although it may take a middle-aged man longer to get an erection, he usually has more control over his eventual ejaculation than when he was younger. And if an older man ejacu-lates *only when he really wants to*, he can continue having regular intercourse indefinitely.

Older women may take longer to secrete vaginal lubrication, but adequate sexual foreplay can bring it on. And although older women may have short and less frequent orgasms, the experience can be fully satisfying. Thus, if we're aware of these and other changes, we can continue pleasurable sex as long as we're alive.

Dr. Alvin Goldfarb, geriatric psychiatrist at Mount Sinai School of Medicine, New York City, and former New York State consultant on service to the aged, said: "increased understanding of one's needs and how they may be suitably gratified can lead to a decrease in sexual or other tensions and convert a person who is searching restlessly for assistance—because he feels helpless and anxious—to one who feels relatively capable, confident, and self-sufficient."

For every "problem" or "inadequacy" we may think we have as we grow older, there is an answer for both mind and body. Dr. John F. O'Connor, of the International Institute for the Study of Human Reproduction, says that the most important factor in maintaining sexual activity into old age is regular sexual expression in earlier years. He adds: "There is no foundation at all for the belief that one can 'use up' sexual capacity, and that abstinence in youth will lead to prolonged years of activity later on. The opposite is true."

Dr. O'Connor also suggests that there is no reason to assume that a person who hasn't achieved a full measure of sexual satisfaction in earlier years won't enjoy sex in older age. He says that short-term sexual therapy can help all of us to find new means of sexual expression and fulfillment. He adds: "We can encourage older people to lead full and satisfying lives, and to include sex among their pleasures in whatever ranking they choose."

Health, Sexuality, and Body Chemistry

The ancient Greeks and Romans stressed a sound mind and a sound body to assure sexual functioning and to defy aging. They felt that health, beauty, and sexuality were links in living, one rarely existing without the others. Sex makes you beautiful at any age; beauty makes you sexy; health creates both and thrives most when both are present.

The keys to good health—and good sex—are adequate rest, exercise, and diet. If you're in normal good health, you'll get all the vitamins and minerals you need by eating a well-balanced diet including meats (especially liver), seafood, dairy products, enriched breads and cereals, dark yellow and green leafy vegetables, beans, peas, citrus fruits, vegetable oils, and iodized salt.

Good sleep and good sex go together. Both involve strong fantasy and the ability to relax. Although sex is not necessarily a sedative in every case (the relaxation period after orgasm lasts only four to five minutes), sexual frustration or tension can keep you awake.

Dr. Harold Lief, professor of psychiatry and director of the Division of Family Study at the University of Pennsylvania School of Medicine, says he determines whether or not a man is physiologically or psychologically impotent by asking him whether he has ever awakened with an erection—even if he can't achieve one in attempted intercourse. If the patient has erections during sleep, his impotence is not physically caused.

In considering exercise, let's admit that the older we get the less likely we are to engage in the formal or planned varieties. We may prefer bending an elbow to lifting wieghts. But many activities and sports we enjoy—such as walking, swimming, cycling, dancing, gardening—involve most of the muscles, and are continuous and rhythmic—the perfect activities to keep us feeling and looking better.

Don't overlook the enjoyable exercise of sexual activity. Dr. Abraham Friedman, a specialist in metabolic diseases and obesity, estimates that the average lovemaking session burns about 200 calories. From the case histories he describes, many overweight people substitute food for sexuality.

Hormones Can Make You Healthy and Happy . . . and Sick

The word "hormone" means "the arouser." A hormone is a body-made chemical, manufactured within a gland, entering the body through blood or lymph, and starting some specific action by cells in other parts of the body. As noted earlier, the sex glands continue to produce hormones—androgen in the male, estrogen in the female—long after the normal reproductive period has ended. We need those hormones to feel alert and alive.

When a woman goes through the climateric or change of life (see Chapter V), her ovaries decrease their estrogen output. She may experience uncomfortable symptoms (usually a hot flash with sweating) because of the estrogen drop and new hormonal balance. Estrogen loss also causes some regression of breast tissue, although this doesn't alter the appearance of the breasts until much later. The tissues of the vulva become thinner and less elastic, the vaginal passage narrows, and the vagina tends to become less acidic. These changes often lead to itching, burning, infections, and pain during intercourse. Application of artificial estrogen (cream, tablets, or suppositories) can help alleviate these conditions.

Estrogen-replacement therapy became popular in the 1960's not only to help a woman through menopause, but to maintain her well-being in later years. A prominent gynecologist, Dr. Robert A. Wilson, maintains that when you find a woman of sixty looking and acting like one in her forties, the chances are that she has had estrogen-replacement therapy. However, a study made by the Boston Collaborative Drug Surveillance Program reveals that the estrogen-taking woman runs a 2.5 times greater risk of developing gallbladder trouble than those who do not take estrogen.

Most physicians will not prescribe supplemental estrogen unless a woman exhibits definite estrogen deficiency, because there is danger in improper treatment. Successful hormone therapy depends upon the physician's knowledge and his ability to recognize endocrine-deficiency disorders.

Physicians sometimes combine estrogen with androgen[1] to create strong feelings of well-being in women. However, too much male hormone may do more harm than good. In a classic case some years ago, a gynecologist administered androgen to stop a woman's uterine bleeding. He stopped the bleeding all right, but the male hormone caused a side effect—it increased the woman's sex drive. She "calmed down" only after the doctor discontinued the androgen and counteracted it with female hormones.

Doctors have used male hormones to enhance libido in women who once enjoyed sex but had since become frigid. They have done so, however, only when the frigidity was secondary; that is, when the patients weren't frigid in the past but had psychologically lost their libido.

Like some aphrodisiacs described in the last chapter, however, hormone-replacement therapy often rests on wishful thinking. When a synthetic drug for the male sex hormone testosterone[2] was first introduced at the Johns Hopkins Hospital some thirty years ago, a fifty-five-year-old technician, who had lost his sexual powers, injected himself with the drug in a controlled scientific experiment. On the day after his first injection, the technician happily reported that his sexual powers had been restored. A month later he felt he needed another injection to maintain his sexual vigor. This time, however, the doctors injected sterile oil (without the drug), although it was taken from a bottle clearly marked "testosterone." The technician reported that the second injection worked as well as the first, if not better. And he reported that he felt renewed after each subsequent injection of the sterile oil. Again, mind over matter.

As with any treatment, hormone therapy has bad as well as good sides. Some hormones could be partly responsible for the development of cancer. Thus, a physician must weigh the good with possible side effects before he administers hormones.

Monkey, Steer, and Goat Glands = Cell Therapy

It's not so great a jump from hormone replacement to cell therapy and gland transplants. In cell therapy, doctors inject embryonic animal organs into the body on the theory that the injected cells will migrate to the same organ in the aging body and reactivate

---

[1] *Androgen* is a male hormone produced by the testes and, to a lesser extent, by the adrenal cortex in both sexes, which is responsible for development of the characteristics associated with maleness.
[2] *Testosterone* is one of the androgens produced by the testes (and the adrenal cortex).

it. Thus, embryonic animal kidney cells could reactivate a human kidney.

In gland transplants, an animal gland is expected to replace or revitalize a human gland. Gland transplants got their start from an Austrian physician, Eugen Steinach, who theorized that if he could block the flow of sperm-producing cells in the testicles, the spermatozoa would back up and stimulate a greater hormone flow into the blood.

He performed his initial operation in 1918 on an aged-looking coachman. Eighteen months later Steinach recorded that the man had a smooth, unwrinkled face, a smart and upright bearing, and looked like a young man at the height of his virility.

Although Steinach's "rejuvenation" was not essentially sexual, it soon became associated with restoring sexual vigor. Steinach's technique was refined by the monkey- and goat-gland transplants of the Russian physician Serge Voronoff. His original idea was to use human donors, but when he found only two volunteers, who further wanted a fortune for their gonads, Voronoff huffed: "At those prices only a millionaire could afford the operation." Thus, he had to settle for the sex glands of monkeys from the equatorial forests of central and western Africa. Even then the operation, using only four strips of monkey gland, cost a minimum of $5,000.

His operation seemed successful to some of his clients, although many had to come back every two years for "retreads." The greatest tragedy was that some of his patients became infected with syphilis— contracted from the monkeys!

Voronoff was befriended by a Swiss doctor, Paul Niehans, who recognized the possibilities of Voronoff's procedures but believed that the glands should be from steers or preferably from sheep, because they are more disease-resistant. Niehans also noted that Voronoff's implants were lined with silk, which rarely took. He made a small pocket without silk, and his transplants took.

Niehans perfected his technique on charity cases, but soon his fame spread, attracting such famous patients as Pope Pius XII, Conrad Adenauer, Theodor Heuss, King Abdul-Aziz ibn-Saud, Thomas Mann, Aga Kahn, III, Gayelord Hauser, Lillian Gish, W. Somerset Maugham, Christian Dior, Bernard M. Baruch, Ann Miller, Gloria Swanson, and others.

Dr. Niehans also tried cell therapy to cure homosexuality, cancer, and diabetes, with negative or inconclusive results.

Niehans died recently, but his clinic still thrives on the shores of

Lake Geneva. There, patients usually spend eight days for eight injections, which cost about $2,000. Europe now has about 5,000 cell therapists who charge anywhere from $100 to $2,000 for treatments.

The cell therapists claim that their injections revitalize elderly minds as well as bodies. Most claims for cell therapy come from studies financed by Niehans himself. Some scientists believe, however, that treatment of biological ailments with biological measures deserves more thorough exploration, and that Niehans opened the door to further research.

Among the problems in cell therapy are the facts that treatments vary and no one is sure how they work. In some cases, therapists use suppositories that aren't actually cells, but antibodies in serum form, obtained from animals that have been injected with appropriate cells. This treatment rests on the theory that it is not the cells themselves that travel to the afflicted organ, but antibodies produced in the blood to attack foreign material that has been injected. It is these antibodies that are supposed to revitalize the cells.

Procaine, Novocain, or Just Plain Gerovital?

Gerovital is another controversial but promising drug therapy. Composed largely of the standard anesthetic procaine, it is similar to Novocain.

Gerovital was developed in the 1950's by a Rumanian physician, Dr. Ana Aslan, after she injected procaine into a young patient whose leg was locked stiff with arthritis. The injection enabled the patient to walk again. Dr. Aslan then tried the drug on older arthritic patients and found that it renewed physical and mental abilities, improved memory, and eased depression. Dr. Aslan then refined her procaine product to reduce side effects and marketed the preparation under the name of Gerovital H3. The product is now essentially a 2 percent solution of procaine hydrochloride whose stability has been improved by processing.

Since introducing Gerovital more than twenty years ago, Dr. Aslan has treated thousands of Europeans including Nikita S. Khrushchev, Sukarno, Ho Chi Minh, Marlene Dietrich, and Viscount Montgomery of Alamein. In his old age, Konrad Adenauer took both cell and Gerovital therapy, which he claimed kept him alert and active.

Dr. Aslan was quickly termed "Dr. Faust in skirts" for her claims that Gerovital could "cure" such old-age complaints as arthritis, arteriosclerosis, eczema, wrinkled skin, baldness, gray hair, loss of appetite, heart disease, neuritis, Parkinson's disease—and impotence!

Critics are quick to note that in addition to the Gerovital injections, Dr. Aslan gives her patients regular physical examinations, a well-balanced diet, intellectual activity, and entertainment. They maintain that this care alone—without the injections—accounts for many good results.

Preliminary results of studies on Gerovital indicate that it has had some success in relieving depression in aging subjects, that it delays aging in cultured cells (obtained from mouse tissue), and that it has few if any adverse side effects.

Although more than 100 imitations of Gerovital (including oral versions) are currently sold in Europe and England, Gerovital cannot be legally obtained in the United States. Clinical studies were conducted here some years ago, but they were discontinued. In May, 1973, however, the F.D.A. authorized the Rom-Amer Co. of Beverly Hills, California, to initiate studies to prove its safety and effectiveness in treating mental depression.

Although Gerovital has not gained complete acceptance and has been called a "phony Fountain of Youth" in an American Medical Association journal, Dr. Aslan was honored at a dinner attended by the then F.D.A. director, Dr. Charles C. Edwards.

The Miracle Drug Is a Chimera

Besides the more dubious elixirs examined in the last chapter, millions of elderly people are seeking their Fountain of Youth in some over-the-counter products available at most drugstores. According to a recent U.S. drug study, people between the ages of forty-five and sixty-four spend at least twice as much for medications as do younger people; after age sixty-five the ratio rises to nearly three to one. And the U.S. Department of Health, Education, and Welfare reports that older people fill and refill more prescriptions than younger people, and they pay more for them.

Irving Ladimer, special counsel/health programs, American Arbitration Association, says: "Without question, the elderly are prime prospects for thousands of items, wondrously named and glowingly promoted, for the conditions which searchers for the Fountain of Youth seem to suffer in abundance. Reports of the F.D.A., F.T.C., and the Post Office Department compiled on cases of deception, fraud, and misrepresentation, place health faddism and fakery at the top of the list."

In the frenzied search for potency through drugs, some older people may take drugs that have adverse effects. Dr. Emil F. Pascarelli, director of community health services of the Roosevelt Hospital, New York City, says that, contrary to public belief, drugs are a problem for the elderly. Besides the heroin and morphine addicts, other elderly people may turn to barbiturates and other depressants such as Valium and Librium—which actually diminish sexual performance.

Most doctors feel that a person's capacity to handle liquor diminishes after age forty, and that some middle-aged and older people develop an allergic reaction to alcohol that can be fatal. One doctor described the extra dry martini as "the quick blow to the back of the neck."

Alcohol increases the desire but diminishes the performance, because it is a depressant—not a stimulant. It may *seem* to increase sexual desire because it blocks inhibitions. It reminds me of a story a friend told about a visit to a bar in Hollywood, California. He was alone in the bar when in walked this woman who sat next to him. She had bleached hair, heavy makeup, and painted nails. About the only natural things about her were the dark circles under her eyes. No matter; after the first drink they became fast friends. After the second drink they were going to be great lovers. After the third drink they were going to be terrific sex partners. After the fourth drink she passed out.

Alcohol may potentiate (intensify) the effect of a hypnotic drug, so that a person taking a drink and then a sleeping pill—even an over-the-counter sleeping aid—will most likely sleep sounder or get a lot drunker, thus diminishing sexual performance. Alcohol may also affect your sexual performance if you are taking cold tablets containing antihistamine or tranquilizers (the same effect as sleeping tablets).

So if you're taking more than one drug or a drug with alcohol, ask your physician or pharmacist if you are interfering with desired actions or exposing yourself to adverse double reactions—such as diminished sexual performance.

When a Fellow/Gal Needs a Lift

Can you identify this actress? She was just another Hollywood starlet who wasn't going anywhere. She had a beautiful body but only a pretty face with a weak chin. One day she went to a plastic surgeon and explained: "I'm no actress and with this chin of mine, I forget my lines if the camera moves in on profile."

The plastic surgeon agreed to correct her weak chin with a simple 15-minute operation in which he would insert a small piece of bone to prop up her chin. With the new chin and renewed confidence, the starlet took a screen test for a major picture and walked away with the part—and into history. Her name was Marilyn Monroe.

There may be times when we feel we need or want a "lift"—and not just for structural defects. The skin starts to show its age somewhere around the late thirties. It starts to lose its elasticity and flexibility and becomes somewhat thinner. Little lines (not yet wrinkles) begin to show—usually the "crow's-feet" around the eyes.

This wrinkling takes place at different times with different people. Heredity may play a part. For instance, one family may have the trait of "wrinkling" around the mouth rather than the eyes. In another family, wrinkling or crow's-feet may start early and then stop.

Although wrinkles don't hurt, you may want to do something about them. One method is *dermabrasion*, or "planing" of the skin. This procedure should be done by a skilled physician, as it consists of spraying on a local anesthetic and then scraping the skin with a motor-driven wire brush or other abrasive tool.

The treatment usually is completed in one session, and you can go home afterward. Any swelling or scab formation usually clears up in about a week or ten days.

In another method, *cryotherapy*, a doctor freezes the skin with carbon dioxide. This induces peeling, which removes shallow wrinkles and improves appearance. Another method applies cauterizing chemicals, which are neutralized when they have obtained the desired action. *A note of caution:* All these techniques can be hazardous, so be sure you have them done by a skilled physician or dermatologist.

Besides wrinkling, the skin becomes more thin, leathery, and darkened as you move toward the forties and fifties. You can tone up your skin with cold cream and other emollients that provide moisture and oil. And avoid overexposure to the sun—one of the prime skin agers.

Cosmetic surgery is becoming increasingly popular and sophisticated for both men and women. Cosmetic surgery includes rhinoplasty (nose), facial plasty (face lift), and breast augmentation and reduction.

Those operations cost from $500 to more than $2,000 depending upon the procedure and the surgeon's reputation. Interestingly, the typical patient for cosmetic surgery—as reported by a survey of plastic surgeons—is a woman around forty-five whose children are grown and who may be widowed or job-hunting (or afraid of losing her husband). The man might be a middle-aged executive who wants to enhance his social or business life.

Doctors perform most such operations under local anesthetics; they take one or more hours, and pain and discomfort are minimized in twenty-four to forty-eight hours. The patient usually resumes work after a few days.

To lift their sex life, more and more women are going in for augmentation mammoplasty. This operation was perfected in Japan after World War II, when the GI's convinced the ladies that men preferred large breasts. From the ladies' standpoint, almost 80 percent report an increase in sex and orgasm, and nearly 80 percent report a greater desire for breast play.

In this operation, a plastic surgeon enlarges a woman's breasts by implanting a gel-like sac of silicone against the chest wall where scar tissue forms and permits firm adhesion. Costs vary from $1,000 to $4,000; $1,500 is average.

The gel implants are much safer than the outdated silicone injections, which were capable of causing infection and of migrating to the upper or lower abdomen.

One woman, in her late forties, told me what was involved in this operation. She said that after going through a medical history and intense questioning as to why she wanted the operation, she checked into a hospital, where she shared a room with another patient.

The doctor showed her boxes containing the various pouches he could use: small, medium, and large. As this woman was in her forties, they agreed that "medium" would be best. She said the pouch was shaped like a teardrop, with a flat back, and was filled with a clear jelly.

The doctor explained that he would make a small incision under each breast and ease the pouch under the fatty tissue and under the milk glands.

She went into surgery (under a general anesthetic), and when she awoke she looked down to see her breasts looming high above her. At this point they were protected by foam and rubber strips. But when she was unwrapped, she was pleasantly surprised to see two beautiful, veined breasts.

"At first I thought they were rather too firm to the touch," she said, "but the doctor assured me that the firmness would disappear as the skin and tissue stretched to accommodate the inserts. And after a few months my breasts became completely soft and natural to the touch.

"I can wear any kind of clothing or appear totally nude, and no one can tell. There is a small scar, less than an inch, about one inch above the natural fold of the breast on the rib cage. If I go bra-less, I jiggle, but less than natural breasts would."

Doctors can remove, replace, or exchange these implants. And even women in small towns are having this operation. My informant added: "My sexual response to breast caressing is now normal and wonderful. I'm not limited to only certain clothing styles; a bathing suit or a bathrobe curves in the expected places. I feel like a new woman!"

The Food and Drug Administration stopped the practice of enlarging breasts by injecting liquid silicone, considering it too hazardous. If any physician (except eight United States physicians who are specially licensed) is injecting soft tissue with liquid silicone, he may be using commercial silicone, which is neither pure nor sterile. French and Japanese silicone is usually medically pure, and doctors in Tokyo, Paris, and Rio de Janeiro have performed face lifts by injecting liquid silicone to fill in the wrinkles and lines.

Unfortunately, not all plastic surgeons are good artists. A famous surgeon, Dr. Mario Gonzalez-Ulloa of Mexico City says: "The contemporary plastic surgeon, even if he is well trained, still lacks an appreciation of beauty ... Properly executed, the reconstruction should reflect in the patient's eyes his or her new identity as a normal human personality."

Another famous plastic surgeon, Dr. Maxwell Maltz, discovered that although he could make people look great on the outside, they often still felt terrible on the inside. "It opened a whole new horizon to me," he said. "I came to realize that the inner scars were far more disabling to more people, but that they could remove them with a little compassion and respect for themselves."

The trouble with some lifts is that your friends and lovers may not recognize you with your "character" lines removed or altered. And with a face lift, you may be looking at the world with a wrinkle-free but masklike visage.

A good personality lift may be better than a face lift or bust lift. And a good spiritual overhaul may be more image-enhancing than a nose lift.

What Your Doctor Should Tell You About Sex—But Can't

A middle-aged friend of mine had a heart attack. His doctor gave him careful instructions about daily activities. But when my friend asked timidly about marital relations, the doctor brushed him off with: "Just take it easy."

The sad part is that many physicians are unwilling or unable or too busy to deal frankly and factually with sexual problems. However, one survey showed that 15 percent of all patients seeing a general practitioner do so for specific sexual problems, and many persons in their sixties and seventies ask about the effect of an operation or treatment on their sex lives.

In a survey made by the late Dr. Ethel Nash, a professor of medicine at Wake Forest College, North Carolina, doctors ranked "poor sexual adjustment" as the main complaint brought to them. Yet only one out of four of these doctors said he discussed sex problems with his patient—and only then if the patient raised the subject first.

Dr. Eric Pfeiffer, professor of psychiatry at Duke University, says he has found that older people *aren't* particularly hesitant about discussing sexual matters, but that some young medical investigators are. He adds: " . . . we found that they (investigators) could not bring themselves to ask any questions about sex of elderly women who had never been married . . . it wasn't until we put our questions into the form of a self-administered questionnaire that we were able to get information about sexual behavior of unmarried women."

"The family doctor is on a pedestal," says Dr. David Reed, assistant director of the Center for the Study of Education in Medicine, "but he's just as much of a 'pretend' sex expert—and just as uptight about the emotional and moral aspects of sex—as anyone else."

Dr. Lonny Myers, vice-president of the Midwest Association for the Study of Human Sexuality, lists these "frauds" as being promulgated by some respected doctors: (1) marital sex is best (healthiest); (2) extramarital sex is bad (unhealthy); (3) casual sex is unhealthy and a sign of neurosis; (4) homosexual behavior is unhealthy and a sign of neurosis; (5) use of sexual appliances is unwise and may destroy normal sexual response; and (6) the double standard is still waving.

One reason for medical hang-ups is that until a few years ago only a handful of medical schools offered any sex-education courses. And medical schools teach students to take medical histories but not sexual histories. Dr. Harold Lief believes that a doctor's stern approach to sexual morality reflects the compulsive and disciplined temperament of the kind of person who enters medicine.

Are there plans to teach sex to doctors as well as patients? The American Medical Association recently published the handbook *Human Sexuality* for its members, and special associations—among them the American Academy of Family Physicians, the American College of Pediatrics, the American College of Obstetrics and Gynecology—have established "continuing education" workshops in sex for their members.

Most medical schools now have courses designed to help students learn about sex. Some use pornographic films to "desensitize" their students. In one such program, the films depicted in the following order: a heterosexual couple making love; a woman masturbating; a man masturbating; a female homosexual couple making love; a male homosexual couple making love; and a pair of frog puppets writhing about.

Dr. Herbert Vandervoort, director of the Human Sexuality Program at the University of California Medical School, said: "The porno stuff is not intended to teach them anything, but to exhaust their fears about looking at pornographic material. When they're through, these fledgling doctors and health practitioners will feel that there's nothing they haven't seen—or couldn't discuss."

However, some programs fail to draw men. In a Nassau County (New York) Community College Course on Family Life and Human Sexuality, women outnumber men three to one, and there's talk that women who want to take the course may be required to bring men with them. Said one professor: "Most males are pigheaded and think they know all there is to know about sex."

If Your Doctor Can't Tell You, Who Can?

Some studies indicate that clergymen see more people with sexual problems than do marriage counselors, psychologists, or doctors.

In one church—the First Baptist Church of San Carlos, California—a minister and his wife operate a church-directed human sexuality workshop. Says the minister-counselor James H. Cox: "Religion has had its part in creating sexual hang-ups, so it's important that the church provides new freedom in this area."

The minister and his wife feel that the main inability of a couple is to deal openly with their feelings. "We concentrate on getting them to request from each other what they need in sexual relations. A man who thinks the roast is overdone never hesitates to tell his wife, but openness stops at the bedroom door."

Dr. Stephen Neiger, a Fellow of the Society for the Scientific Study of Sex, believes in behavior therapy based on learning to resolve sexual problems. He asserts that neurotic symptoms are learned behavior; having learned them, you can unlearn them and learn more desirable behavior patterns.

Behavior therapy centers on the problem, whether it is frigidity, impotence, or fear of penetration, and tries to solve it without delving into the past. When a patient is completely relaxed, he/she is given minimal exposure in words, pictures, and sound to those things he/she is afraid of. The therapist gradually increases the exposure to build up the patient's tolerance. Says Dr. Neiger: "In desensitizing impotency, I may instruct the patient to lie close to his wife for several nights, petting, kissing—just concentrating on the moment without feeling the pressure of attempting intercourse. When the couples are relaxed, the impotency will usually disappear."

Just talking about sexual problems is great therapy. Dr. Sidney R. Saul, New York therapist and consultant in mental health, tells of a group of senile mental patients—with an average age of eighty—who were encouraged to join in a group discussion about sex. Many of the patients hadn't joined in any previous discussions, and most of them were disoriented as to time, place, or event. But all of them joined in this discussion, became lucid and animated, and were aware of their surroundings. The conference was summarized by a man who had not joined in discussions before, and the meeting was adjourned (by announcing time for lunch) by a patient who was usually disoriented.

The "Masters" of the Sex Helpers

The leading sex therapists at present are Dr. William H. Masters and Mrs. Virginia E. Johnson (husband and wife), who are sex researchers and directors of the Reproductive Biology Research Foundation in St. Louis, Missouri. Their work is based on their assumption that " . . . a conservative estimate would indicate that half the marriages in this country are either presently sexually dysfunctional or imminently so in the future."

The Masters and Johnson therapy rests on the idea that

" . . . there is no such thing as an uninvolved partner in any marriage in which there is some form of sexual inadequacy." Thus they treat both husband and wife, and they assert that the average troubled couple over the age of fifty stands a better-than-even chance of reversing their problems.

The research teams of the foundation combine education with psychotherapy. They use dual-sex therapy teams, so that the husband and wife each has a "friend in court" and an "interpreter" of the same sex who can support and explain that person's point of view during the talk sessions.

The dual-sex teams employ "reflective teaching" to show the partners what they really are like, what their problems are, how they are hurting each other, and how they fail to communicate with each other.

Once the patients accept criticism and instruction, they are ready to allow themselves to think and feel about sex as the natural process it is. The therapy removes the "produce, perform, and achieve" pressure from the patients. The first step is to forbid any sexual activity unless directed. Sexual responsiveness comes little by little, building blocks for progress in later phases.

All couples are referred to the foundation by physicians, psychologists, social workers, or clergy. The full fee is around $3,000 for the two-week program and five years of follow-up consultation. Patients pay their own living expenses.

And Then There Are Marriage Counselors

The "twenty-year fracture" is replacing the "seven-year itch." Statistics show that 25 percent or more of today's divorces are among couples married fifteen years and longer, and marriages of twenty, twenty-five, and thirty years are ending in divorce.

If you can't resolve you own marriage difficulties, you can turn to a marriage counselor. This is still an infant art or science, and few states—among them California, Michigan, and New Jersey—require marriage counselors to have a certificate. In most states anyone can hang out a shingle as a marriage counselor and charge as much as $2,000 for his services.

One way to select a marriage counselor is to write for *The Directory of Members of the American Association of Marriage Counselors* ($2) from their offices at 3603 Lemmon Avenue, Dallas, Texas 75219. Any member agency of the Family Service Association of America will probably have well-qualified marriage counselors on its staff and know of competent counselors in private practice.

In the final analysis, it's up to you. What do you think you need and want? Before you rush off to get help because you think you may not be "normal," read the next chapter.

IV
HOW "SEXY" CAN YOU GET?

Years ago, a thick book circulated entitled *Sex After Sixty*. It had an attractive cover and imposing typography. But when you opened the book—the pages were blank!

I remember most peoples' guffaws when they opened the book, but I can also recall my embarrassment (I'm sure others felt the same).

The tricksters, laughers, and blushers overlook the facts of living: sex in the later years isn't written in invisible ink; it's indelibly printed on today and tomorrow. With each passing day, more and more middle-aged and older people are becoming sexually emancipated and active!

For more than twenty years, the Duke University Center for the Study of Aging has been studying the sexual interest and activities of middle-aged and older persons. The findings are vitally important to you and me.

One study involving 261 men and 241 women aged forty-five to sixty-nine found that changes observed in old age had their beginnings in middle age. The findings indicated that whereas we lose some sexual interest and activity as we grow older, sex continues to play a vital role in our lives. Only 6 percent of the men studied and 33 percent of the women said they were no longer interested in sex, and only 12 percent of the men and 44 percent of the women said they no longer had sexual relations.

Interestingly, the oldest age group indicated more sexual involvement than did the next-to-the-oldest group, perhaps because the oldest group consisted of elite survivors.

By age fifty, about half (49 percent) of the men and over half (58 percent) of the women admitted some decline in sexual interest and activity. By age seventy, almost all men (88 percent) and women (96 percent) admitted that they were aware of a decline. The sharpest declines were registered between the age groups forty-five to

59

fifty and fifty-one to fifty-five.

Generally, those with the greatest sexual interest and activity were those who had led active sex lives when younger and were healthier, better adjusted, and better off financially.

In a study of 250 men and women over age sixty, Duke researchers found that sex continued to play an important role in the lives of many persons in their sixties, seventies, eighties, and even nineties. Well over half (60 percent) of married couples between ages sixty to seventy-four remained sexually active, but after age seventy-five less than one-third (30 percent) of married couples had intercourse. Of the single people, only 7 percent continued sexual relations in old age.

Among men in their late sixties, an average 80 percent still indicated active sexual interest; ten years later, in the late seventies, half (50 percent) still had such interest. Furthermore, 70 percent of men in their late sixties were still sexually active; ten years later one-quarter (25 percent) were still regularly sexually active.

Among the women, half (50 percent) indicated active sex interest in their late sixties, declining to about one-third (30 percent) in the late seventies. In their late sixties about one-third (30 percent) still had regular sexual intercourse; in the late seventies this declined to less than one-quarter (20 percent). Interestingly, about 15 percent of the women *showed an increase in sexual interest* as they grew older.

What was the average age that sex stopped for men and women? *About sixty for women and sixty-eight for men.* When the Duke researchers asked the men why they had stopped sex, they blamed declining health, interest, or potency. The women said they had stopped because their husbands had died, become ill, or lost interest or potency. Only one woman said she stopped sex because *she* had lost interest.

Thus, while there is no biological limit to sexual interest and activity of women, *their activity depends upon the survival of their men.* And as women outlive men by seven years—and marry men four to six years older—women are often forced to give up sexual relations sooner than they'd like.

Although the women in the Duke study had lower interest and activity levels, remember that most of them were born before 1900, when sexual attitudes were Victorian. Many women were taught that sex was a biological "duty" that ceased after menopause; to feel "sexy" after age fifty made many women feel guilty and ashamed.

How sad! Older men and women need sex to reinforce themselves physically and mentally. The man needs sex at a time when he's facing the loss of accustomed prestige, and the woman needs sex to prove that she's still desirable (and desirous) after menopause. Stopping sex at this time often hastens old age, causing a self-fulfilling prophecy of the barrenness of the later years.

How much sex do people have? Dr. Elliott M. Feigenbaum, Medical Director, Western Institute of Human Resources quotes statistics to show that the "average" rate of sexual intercourse is 4.8 times per week for young couples, but drops to 1.8 times per week at age fifty, and 1.3 times per week at age sixty.

As we'll discuss later *"averages" are meaningless and don't apply to you and me.* It's up to each of us as to how much sex we need or want. When Dr. Feigenbaum asked a group of 600 persons over the age of sixty how much sex a person that age should have, he got a broad sampling of answers: "Nothing. Rosary beads and go to church" . . . "At least once a week. That will keep you young" . . . "Depends on whether you're happily married and how much vitamin E you eat" . . . "Try weekly" (interviewer, after a long pause "How do you spell that?").

Dr. Pfeiffer of Duke University says: "One of the most important determinants of sexual activity later in life is the level of sexual activity and interest in earlier years. Those with greater sexual activity earlier in life continue to be more active later in life. If you save it, you lose it. It's really that simple."

As They Say, It's All in the Head

"It's all in the head" explains mainly how sex begins as well as ends. To feel sexy you've got to be stimulated in the mind as well as the body. Your erectile nerves have a control center at the base of your spine. To this center come all sorts of stimulating messages: thoughts, memories, fantasies, views of an attractive partner or erotic pictures; pleasant aromas and sounds; touches on sensitive parts of the body.

When the control center receives enough positive messages it signals the penis or clitoris: Let's go! The more stimulating messages your sex organ receives, the more active it wants to become.

Alas, there are the "bad guys"—the fears, anxieties, and hang-ups—you may have about sex. These negative thoughts interfere with positive performance; unless the "good guys" win over the "bad guys," you won't feel sexy. In younger days, the good guys almost always win, but if inhibitions or bad times pile up, the bad guys may head them off at the pass.

Hormones also have their say on whether you become aroused sexually. Further clouding the chemical mix is the fact that it is probably the male hormone—androgen—that stimulates both men and women, because it makes the sex organs more sensitive and responsive. But *it doesn't necessarily follow that adding more hormones will make you any sexier.* If the response threshold is already well primed with hormones, adding more probably won't make much difference. Androgen probably also raises the body's general metabolism and nerve functions, but it's still a case of mind over matter.

Women are particularly sensitive to mental stimulation. Psychologists and lovers know that to arouse a woman, you need the finesse of poetry, the charm of romance, and the loftiness of spirituality. A woman's "sexiness" is so closely related to her emotional life that her sexual organs are more susceptible to such emotions as fear. These fears needn't be conscious: hidden fears cause more sexual difficulties than recognized fears and guilts.

Did We Bring It On Ourselves?

We can blame the kids whom we reared for a lot. We taught them that sex was "dirty," so when they grow up they think we're "dirty" if we get sexy. It reminds me of the remark of Sam Levenson, the schoolteacher and homespun philosopher: "When I first found out how babies were born, I couldn't believe it! To think that my father and mother would do such a thing!" Then after reflection he added: "My father—maybe, but my mother—*never!*"

As we said, what is considered virility at age twenty-five looks like lechery at age sixty-five. Many kids get upset when they see oldsters "carrying on," and the oldsters are afraid to act sexy when the kids are around. Dr. Ewald W. Busse, Chairman of the Department of Psychiatry at Duke University, comments: " . . . it's also possible that the taboo against sex in old age serves the selfish interests of the middle and younger generation. To maintain the stereotype of the elderly as an asexual group or as a group incapable of competing with them in many aspects of living is fostered by young people."

The kids may have a more practical and sinister reason: they may really by worrying about losing an inheritance if they see an unmarried parent (widow or widower) carrying on, and they mask their fear with disapproval.

The kids also have a saying: "Live fast, die young, and leave a beautiful corpse." But perhaps it's not so much old age as *middle age* that the kids want to avoid. Middle age converts our grand ideas to grim determination to hang on to what we've got. When we go from "wild liberalism" to "mature conservatism" we lose the respect of many youngsters.

David P. Ausubel, in *Theory and Problems of Adolescent Development*, notes that transition to aging resembles adolescence: we're in the marginal position of losing an established and accustomed status without acquiring a new one—a stressful situation, to say the least. In middle age some of us become so frightened that we may flee into premature old age, where we won't have to keep fighting for the physical and emotional satisfactions we want. But we may pay for it, both mentally and physically. We've agreed that there is no automatic cutoff date for sex. Yet sex can't flourish in a social climate that dampens sexual expression and an environment that nurtures myths and misconceptions about sex in the later years.

Let's Explode the Myths

I interviewed many prominent doctors and sifted the findings of the Sex Information and Education Council of the U.S. (SIECUS) to explode the following myths and explore some truths:

1. *Abstinence in youth and middle age will enable you to "save yourself" for the later years.* The opposite is true. The sexier you were when younger, the sexier you'll be when older. Sex keeps the hormone level up; people who enjoy sex more are less subject to fatigue than others. An occasional orgasm is like sipping at the well spring of life.

2. *Intercourse is weakening and will hasten old age.* Doctors point out that the emission of semen is no more of a loss than is the loss of saliva. Before semen is discharged, it has already been stored in the organs and is "out of circulation." After discharge, it is quickly replaced by the body. During self-stimulation a woman may experience as many as twenty orgasms before becoming satiated. Masters and Johnson concluded that the average woman could continue such stimulation for an hour or more and reach as many as fifty orgasms. Thus, neither ejaculation nor orgasm "deplete" the body.

3. *After menopause a woman can't enjoy sex physically or emotionally.* Often the opposite is true. A woman may enjoy a "second honeymoon" because she doesn't have to worry about becoming pregnant. Even after a hysterectomy, a woman's sex level

remains and may even increase.

4. *The man is sexually superior to the woman.* Biologically and psychologically, the opposite is probably true. In childbearing days, it is probably the woman's vaginal contractions that pulls in the sperm, rather than the man's ejaculation. During the sex act, the woman can have multiple orgasms, whereas the man usually has only one and needs minutes, hours, or even days before he can have another.

5. *Simultaneous orgasms.* Merely knowing that a woman is capable of multiple orgasms should make a man realize that she should have several before he has his "final" orgasm. One woman who had been married for twenty-two years told how she used to "hold off," believing that she should have only one orgasm with her husband. It was only until she learned that she could (and should) have multiple orgasms that she really began to enjoy sex.

6. *The vaginal orgasm.* From a biological point of view clitoral and vaginal orgasms are not separate. Doctors point out that the lower one-third of the vagina and the clitoris activate the female orgasm, and that both should be stimulated to bring on orgasm. Interestingly, scientists maintain that the clitoris is not a small penis, but that the penis is more like an enlarged clitoris!

7. *The ideal position for sex.* Regardless of position, the penis rarely comes in contact with the clitoris. Thus, various positions to increase penile contact are superfluous or impossible. However, there is more direct contact in female-on-top and side-by-side positions. And regardless of position, there must be some direct or indirect stimulation of the clitoris. (For more on "techniques," see Chapter IX.)

8. *The superiority of the large penis.* The vagina can accommodate any size of penis. Doctors say it's a fallacy to assume that the larger penis is better able to stimulate the clitoris; it's the stimulation, not the size, that counts.

9. *Creativity is a sublimation of sex.* Many men and women may tend to deny or sublimate their sexual urges by plunging into business, cultural events, or affairs of church or state. But Dr. Leon Salzman, professor of clinical psychiatry at Georgetown University School of Medicine, points out that psychologists believe that forces other than sex govern our aesthetic, artistic, and philosophic pursuits. He adds: "Creativity is the outcome of the fullest expression of man's total capacities and ideals, not simply a sublimation of sex."

What Happens to Men as They Grow Older?

Men have more of an "identity crisis" than women. A man's sexual drive centers in a simple biological act: erection and ejaculation. As he grows older, he may find it harder to achieve an erection and harder to ejaculate. Also, a man's most masculine part is his most vulnerable.

Regardless of age, a man has four sexual stages: (1) *excitement* (getting an erection); (2) *plateau* (increasing excitement to maintain erection); (3) *orgasm* (ejaculation); and (4) *resolution* (he's "had it"). Whereas a middle-aged man may take longer to achieve an erection, a man of sixty or over may not get a full erection until just before ejaculation.

But this has its advantages. The man can prolong the excitement stage to please himself and his partner. And although his ejaculation stage may blend into one stage rather than two, he can still "come" when he really wants and needs to. Masters and Johnson have proven that *if a man ejaculates only when he really desires to,* he can have sex regularly, indefinitely. As you grow older you may think you want sex more than you really desire it; if you're having any problems, wait until you really *want* sex. Strive for quality, not quantity.

Masters and Johnson also pinpointed men's reasons for declining sexual interest in later years:

1. *Monotonous sexual relations.* Many men feel they need or want sexual variety to make life interesting. One recent study of call girls showed that their older customers wanted oral-genital and other forms of uninhibited sex. It's true that in most cases husbands have perfected a "comfortable" but mainly routine method of sexual expression. Without variety and surprises, sex then becomes routine —and monotonous. Dr. Jesse Bernard, a noted sexologist, says: "Conservative, middle-class men often behave as though sex were no longer either interesting or dynamic. They may rechannel their own interest into risque stories, joking, and horseplay. Feeling that they all share the same problem, they face it at least with a show of outer resignation if not always with inner equanimity. There is simply little stimulation in a relationship which has become routinized."

2. *Preoccupation with the job.* Most men between the ages of forty and sixty are locked into their careers, either making one last frenzied attempt at "fame and fortune" or trying desperately to hang onto what they have. When things go wrong at work, they become preoccupied, and this preoccupation curses sexual interest.

3. *Mental and physical fatigue.* Along with preoccupation, men-

tal and physical fatigue curbs sexual appetite. If a desk-bound male tries to become a weekend athlete, his physical fatigue piles on top of his mental fatigue, knocking him out of the box for twenty-four to forty-eight hours.

4. *Too much food and drink.* Excess eating and drinking curbs sexual appetites. A heavy meal makes you sleepy; too many drinks deadens performance. In fact, Masters and Johnson blame alcohol as the *number-one killer of sexual performance.* Unfortunately, many men are unaware that the alcohol is to blame, and they may drink more out of frustration. They may also chase women who are not aware of their problem, in hopes that the "thrill" of a new conquest will resolve impotence. If they can perform (and/or if they drink less), they may think it's the new partner, not the reduced drinking that is the solution. The tragedy, say Frederick Lemere and James W. Smith, writing in the *American Journal of Psychiatry,* is that sexual impotency stemming from alcohol abuse may last even after years of sobriety. They state: "The problem is neither a psychological nor a hormonal defect but is due to the destructive effect of alcohol on the neurogenic reflex arc that serves the process of erection. The damage may be irreversible, accounting for the inability of some men to reattain potency."

5. *Physical handicaps.* Any physical disability, acute or chronic, usually lowers the sexual drive. If a man has an acute illness such as pneumonia, he will probably start feeling sexier as he recovers. But if he has a chronic problem such as emphysema or diabetes, he may remain impotent unless medical treatment curbs the illness and restores the hormonal balance (see Chapter VIII).

6. *Fear of failure.* It has been said that " . . . a man's saddest moment isn't the first time he find he can't do it a second time, but the second time he finds he can't do it the first time." Whatever the circumstances, once impotent, a man may withdraw from sex rather than face the ego-shattering experience of repeated failures. Not infrequently, the man may invent excuses for sexual withdrawal rather than face the facts. But once a man withdraws from regular sexual relations, he hastens aging. *Sex stimulates health and well-being; health and well-being stimulate sex—and retard aging.*

What Happens to Women as They Grow Older?

The menopause (see Chapter V) brings mixed blessings to women. On the one hand, it relieves them of the fear of becoming pregnant and opens the possibilities for a second honeymoon; on the other, it may occasion the notion that sex after menopause has no social value and therefore should be discouraged.

Even if a woman wants more sex after the menopause, her husband probably wants less. Usually he is four to six years older than she, and he may be suffering from some of the problems discussed in the previous section. This is ironic: in earlier days her husband wanted more sex; now that she wants more sex, he doesn't . . . perhaps in some part due to the fact that she rebuffed his earlier attempts.

Sex researchers say that a woman's lower sexual activity in her fifties and sixties results more from the man's lack of desire than hers. One woman said it didn't seem fair that she was left in the lurch, and that she wanted to launch a "Society for the Chronological Role-Reversal of Emancipated Womanhood"—or SCREW for short.

Women also complain about a boring sex routine. One woman said that her husband completely ignored her until he got into bed, but then she could predict his every word and gesture. She added: " . . . If he changed that routine I'd be so surprised I probably would have a stroke or laugh or something. Sex isn't an adventure . . . it hasn't been for twenty years . . . "

Although a man may rejuvenate his sex life by taking a new young, attractive partner, a woman finds it harder to attract a younger male. Writer Susan Sontag calls this the "double standard of aging" and said that as a man grows "older but wiser" he has "character lines," but a woman merely gets wrinkles. Ms. Sontag adds: "Widowed or divorced, a man is usually considered more sexually attractive and more eligible for remarriage at a later age."

Women can learn new sexual techniques to stimulate themselves and their partners (see Chapter IX). Billie Jo Starr, in *I Hate Sex*, suggests maybe a "hot session of oral or manual stimulation to do the trick." Or she advises playing up to a man's ego so he'll feel needed and wanted. "Reassure him that he's still your big, strong knight in shining armor . . . That sort of manure is the best fertilizer in the world to make the limp weed of his virility grow straight and strong again."

What of the woman who finds herself a sudden widow (or divorcée) with no available sex partner? The Masters and Johnson studies show that many women substitute masturbation for the sexual activity they used to have with their partners; and Kinsey reported on one woman of ninety who masturbated to orgasm regularly.

Certainly, masturbation would seem to be preferable to some outlets I've seen. I recall going into a bar in St. Petersburg, Florida, at about 5 P.M. and seeing two ladies, widows in their fifties or sixties, sitting at the bar. After a couple of drinks, I discovered that they were there to "meet people" . . . perhaps not for sex, but for a "good time." One woman claimed that all she was looking for was "drinks and dinner," with perhaps a "good-night kiss" to end the evening. It reminded me of Friday nights in my younger days in San Francisco, when a girl might hope that two drinks would lead to more drinks and dinner, but a man hoped that it would lead to anything but drinks and dinner. Anyhow, these ladies were playing a dangerous game at best; if they had a real sex urge, they might have been better off doing something about it at home rather than taking chances of getting a disease or a beating from a pickup.

What's the Hang-up About Masturbation?

Dr. Lester W. Dearborn, marriage consultant, in pointing out the role masturbation plays in the lives of the single or widowed, comments: "It is to be hoped that those interested in the field of geriatrics will . . . encourage the aging to accept masturbation as a perfectly valid outlet when there is a need and other means of gratification aren't available."

Many sex counselors told me that although older people might need and want to masturbate when no other valid outlet was present, they often needed reassurance to accept the practice.

In a study made by *Sexology* magazine some years ago of men listed in *Who's Who in America*, about one-fourth of the men (most of them married) reported masturbating after age sixty. Another study of married women showed that about 30 percent masturbated at age fifty and 25 percent at age sixty-five. Widows and divorcées doubled these rates. Yet many of these women still have hang-ups about the subject.

One doctor told of a seventy-three-year-old widow who sought medical help to "cure her" of this practice. And another doctor reported several cases of women between the ages of sixty and eighty who sought professional advice to "fight against their worst selves."

Men also have problems with masturbation. An eighty-five-year-old man who could no longer have sex with his ill wife said: "My own moral and religious sense, coupled with a sense of self-respect, keeps me from masturbation. It certainly isn't lack of sexual desire."

Why these hang-ups? Our own condemning attitude reflects the Judeo-Christian tradition that "wasting seed" violates the command-ment to "increase and multiply." This dogma influenced church and state thinking for centuries; in our country, the states of Indiana and Wyoming have ruled that inducing another person to masturbate is sodomy.

Until the early part of this century, medical opinion reinforced the widely held beliefs in the "evils" of masturbation. Prestigious doctors held "masturbation clinics," and medical supply houses sold aluminum mitts and even "chastity belts" to prevent children from "self-abuse." Although most medical warnings were directed at males, the clamor against female masturbation was so intense that sometimes clitoroidectomy (removal of the clitoris) was performed.

Medical opinion now agrees that masturbation—no matter how frequently practiced—produces none of the physical effects warned about in the past. Physicians say that the physical effects of mastur-bation are no different than the physical effects of any sexual activity, that masturbation can be considered excessive only in the same light that too much reading or TV-watching might be con-sidered excessive.

Why and How Do People Masturbate?

Dr. David Reuben, author of *How to Get More Out of Sex*, says that "therapeutic masturbation" plays a vital role in overcoming male impotence and female orgasmic impairment. He adds: "Like practicing tennis strokes against a backboard, in its ideal form sexual solitaire is simply playing a one-handed game to learn how to play better with a partner."

Also, men have a biological urge to release semen at regular intervals. Given the simplicity of their sex organs and of ejaculation, most men just hand-manipulate the penis. Some may rub up against bedclothes, pillows, or other objects. There is also a device for masturbation, a foam-rubber stretch-stocking with a series of tiny built-in vibrators that fits over the penis. Flip a switch, and the penis is alternately squeezed and released about a hundred times a minute. Like many other devices, this one is potentially dangerous—even fatal.

Masturbation has become increasingly common with women because, as Masters and Johnson researchers have found, the act usually causes even more intense uterine contractions than does sexual intercourse. Through masturbation, a woman can discover what does and doesn't stimulate her sexually. Masturbation also releases tensions and stimulates sexual appetite in woman.

Sexual intercourse isn't even a very reliable index of the time it takes for a woman to reach orgasm. When masturbating, most women are able to climax in about three to four minutes—fairly close to the average male rate.

A woman's anatomy allows considerable variety in masturbation. Most women caress the entire genital region, using the hand or one, two, or three fingers to stimulate the shaft of the clitoris and the inner lips of the vagina. They may also use thigh-rubbing, pressing together or crossing the legs and squeezing the inner muscles of the thigh, bringing pressure on the vagina lips and indirectly on the clitoris. Many women combine clitoral stimulation with breast manipulation to reach orgasm; some women can reach orgasm through breast manipulation alone.

Other women pull panties, nightgowns, pajamas, or bedsheet between the thighs and rock back and forth to excite the clitoris.

Some women use vibrators to masturbate (Chapter II) and others insert cylindrical objects for that "filled up" feeling. One woman said: "I like having something in my vagina for my contracting muscles to get a grip on. It's better that way." (There is always the danger of objects getting stuck in the vagina.)

Among more sophisticated women, the newest masturbatory "tool" is the flat side of an electric toothbrush held tight against the vagina and clitoris (one woman describes it as "like riding a rail"). Some women use "water manipulation" by directing a stream of water (spray hose, shower, massage pump, even dental jet) at the vaginal region while sitting in the bathtub.

Masturbation positions seem important. One woman said she can lie on the bed and masturbate, but she can't have an orgasm unless she's standing. Others say they like to straddle the edge of the bathtub or a door and rub up and down. Some women masturbate while riding horses; others place a sanitary napkin so that it causes friction on the clitoris.

While most doctors and older persons now accept masturbation as desirable when no other outlets are available, *no one suggests that masturbation replaces satisfactory sexual relationships.* And there is some evidence that masturbation can interfere with satisfactory sexual relations. Doctors have reported that unduly brief intercourse was usually the result of a timing pattern set up by frequent masturbation. Since exactly the same nerve pathways are trained in either activity, timing is also trained, and this can establish a pattern that is satisfactory for auto-erotic activity, but not for a couple's activity. But this pattern can be changed by concentrating on foreplay and not on immediate relief.

Are There Other Sexual Outlets?

Some responsible physicians and social scientists have advocated polygamy after age sixty as a valid sexual outlet. They point out the increasing imbalance in the sexual makeup of the adult population. At age twenty there are 105 females for every 100 males; at age sixty-five the proportion is 138.5 females to every 100 males, and at seventy-five it is 156 females to 100 males.

The aging male can expand his sexual horizons; he has a vast pool of women to draw from. On the other hand, the aging female finds herself increasingly restricted in the choice of men who are attractive or available as sex partners.

About the only way to remedy this, say some prominent scientists, would be to urge that men in their sixties be free to marry two to five women in the same age group. According to some of these advocates, plural marriage would be beneficial by (1) reestablishing a meaningful family group; (2) improving diets; (3) offering the opportunity to pool funds; (4) providing care if one partner became ill; (5) enabling two or more women to share the housework; and (6) solving the problem of not enough partners to go around.

On the other hand, although the man might stimulate his sex interest with a variety of new partners and techniques, a woman might not fare so well. As one woman said: "I'm lonesome, but not that lonesome!"

What Can You Do to Restore That Twinkle in the Eye?

In *The Joy of Sex*, noted British geriatrician Dr. Alex Comfort writes that the longer you love, the more you learn. He adds that stopping sex is like stopping bicycle riding—you do it because you're ill, think it looks silly, or don't have a bicycle. He adds: "Over age 50, the important thing is never to drop sex for any long period—keep yourself going solo if you don't have a partner for the time being; if you let it drop you may have trouble restarting."

It reminds me of the loving couple in their seventies who thought that the time had finally come for twin beds. But as soon as they got the beds, their sexual activity stopped. A friend advised: "If you want old-fashioned loving, you should get an old-fashioned double bed. Twin beds are for twins."

You shouldn't lose any more sexual vigor with age than you do any other physical capacity. You may not be able to run 100 yards as fast as you did, but you can still reach your goal just the same. Just as your body can perform, so is your mind calling the signals. Dr. Paul Cameron, a psychologist at the University of Louisville (Kentucky), says that while sex thoughts cross your mind every ten minutes when you're between ages eighteen and twenty-five, they are still crossing your mind every thirty-five minutes at age forty-five and once an hour at age sixty-five.

Perhaps that is why timing is so important for sex in the later years. Catch your desires at the right moment, and both mind and body will be in tune. Dr. Adel Ismail, of the Endocrinology Research Unit in Edinburgh, Scotland, found that man's highest sexual hormone levels occur between 4 A.M. and noon—while the lowest is at 8 P.M. Also, a man's sex organs function better in a cool climate than in a hot one. So perhaps the cool morning would be a better time to make love than the hot (and probably fatigued) evening.

Also, in later life, let's emphasize the *quality* of life and love rather than the quantity. A mature wife should be a better sex partner than any average woman in her twenties. Albert Ellis, a noted psychologist, says that millions of older women have been able to free themselves from the old notions that various sexual positions and play are perversions. Two British writers, Drs. Kenneth Walker and Eric B. Strauss, say: "There is a disposition on the part of some married couples to feel that while certain methods of lovemaking are right and proper, others are illegitimate or degrading. That which is for them mutually pleasing and satisfying is right; that which to either party seems objectionable is wrong. The schoolmaster and the policeman have no right of entry into the bedroom, for love can recognize, apart from moral law, no rules other than those that it frames for itself."

Although most lovemaking will be "straight," it's nice to plan a little surprise now and then. Perhaps American wives should take lessons from French wives, who maintain certain small reserves and avoid the dangers of too-complete familiarity.

A day at the beach, supper out, candlelight, and wine all add to the environment that makes love flourish—whatever its form.

Love Flourishes Best in Privacy

Like young people, older people want to be alone when they make love. Yet many hospitals, nursing homes, and private homes don't give us the privacy we need and want. Dr. Marion Powell, of the University of Toronto School of Hygiene, said that if homes for the aged set aside petting rooms, "I'd suspect they'd have a long waiting list."

Growing older has a sort of *Alice in Wonderland* quality about it, or is it in *Through the Looking Glass* that Humpty Dumpty says to Alice:

"So here's a question for you. How old did you say you were?"

Alice made a short calculation, and said "Seven years and six months."

"Wrong!" Humpty Dumpty exclaimed triumphantly. "You never said a word like it!"

"I thought you meant 'How old *are* you?'" Alice exclaimed.

"If I'd meant that, I'd have said it," said Humpty Dumpty.

Alice didn't want to begin another argument, so she said nothing.

"Seven years and six months!" Humpty Dumpty repeated thoughtfully. "An uncomfortable sort of age. Now if you'd asked *my* advice, I'd have said 'Leave off at seven'—but it's too late now."

"I never ask advice about growing," Alice said indignantly.

"Too proud?" the other enquired.

Alice felt even more indignant at this suggestion. "I mean," she said, "that one can't help growing older."

"*One* can't, perhaps," said Humpty Dumpty; "but *two* can. With proper assistance, you might have left off at seven."

V
NOT FOR WOMEN ONLY

Menopause can mark a new beginning—not the end—of a woman's sexual life.

Menopause need not mean the end of loving or being loved . . . the end of laughter, sex, sunshine, or birthdays! Menopause can mean the beginning of new sexual freedom and a renewed feeling of well-being and self-confidence.

Why, then, the fears? As a society we have let ourselves inherit a dowdy, miserable, even painful image of menopause. We live in a male-dominated, youth-oriented culture. These negative conditions may create signs and symptoms associated with menopause. At any rate, middle-age and old-age stereotypes complicate this natural, predictable biological change.

The apprehensions come, too, from real situations sometimes accompanying this period of life. The label "change of life" doesn't sound like continuity and confidence in the future; it portends catastrophe. Yet change can mean a new beginning if we manage it. To understand, accept, and then manage change, we first need information.

Men who are sensitive and wise (therefore sexy) need to study and understand women as they never have before, because to most women the *menopause means much more than the end of menstruation*. Whether it brings new beginnings depends as much on the husband's attitudes as the wife's.

What Happens During Menopause?

Menopause is part of living. As a woman grows older, her ovaries produce less and less estrogen. Estrogen, a female hormone, helps to develop secondary sex characteristics and strengthens many systems. From her late twenties forward, a woman's estrogen output declines—ever so slowly—but with no noticeable effects until her forties. Eventually, the low estrogen level (an estrogen-progesterone imbalance) causes monthly bleeding to slow down or become irregular and then stop.

The typical natural menopause usually occurs around age fifty, although it may begin as early as the mid-thirties or as late as the late fifties. It may involve excessive bleeding, skipped periods, scanty periods, and mercurial moods.

When the estrogen level becomes lower, the whole endocrine system—the whole body—knows it. Symptoms differ from woman to woman. About one in five will feel hot flashes and chills, nervousness, insomnia, heart palpitation, dizzy spells, or changing appetite. Most women suffer only some of these symptoms, hot flashes being the most common.

Lack of estrogen also decreases vaginal secretions, dries skin and mucuous membranes, narrows the vagina and makes it shorter and less elastic. The dry vaginal surface can bleed easily. These conditions constitute vaginal atrophy, the second most common characteristic in menopausal women.

Doctors differ on appropriate remedies. Some doctors call menopause an estrogen-deficiency disease and attempt to "cure" it by prescribing estrogen. Others believe that estrogen-replacement therapy must *more than* balance the possible side effects. Symptoms are usually caused—at least in part—by low-level estrogen.

A young woman recalls, "I was in a department store with my mother when all of a sudden she looked faint and was bathed in cold sweat. Soon her white blouse was drenched and clung to her. Through it all I could see her chest heaving while we both tried to maintain some sort of dignity. In a flash, the store manager appeared. Mom sat down—somewhat frightened—and I didn't know what to do to help her. No one ever told me what to do in such a case. The store manager kept asking if he could help, but we were all a bit helpless. After a few minutes, my mother was steady and I drove her home."

Hot flashes bother about 50 percent of menopausal women. Other symptoms include dizzy spells, fatigue, increasing or decreasing appetite, headaches, muscle aches, insomnia, and cramps. Most women experience only a few of these signs.

Dr. John F. O'Connor, of Columbia University, discovered that women generally tolerate the physical symptoms rather than complaining . . . as the folklore suggests. His survey of 680 women showed that only 69 complained of any troublesome symptoms, although examinations revealed more than 6,000 separate causes for discomfort, either serious or minor.

As one woman said: "I saw women complaining, and I thought I would never be so ridiculous. I would just sit there and perspire, if I had to. At times you do feel terribly warm. I would sit and feel the water on my head, and wonder how red I looked. But I wouldn't worry about it, because it is a natural thing, and why get worried about it? I remember one time, in the kitchen, I had a terrific hot flash ... I went to look at myself in the mirror. I didn't even look red, so I thought: 'All right ... the next time I'll just sit there, and who will notice? And if someone notices, I won't even care ...."

A U.S. Public Health Service pamphlet says: "Women who have trouble with the menopause are usually those who have nothing to do with their time. Women generally feel better after the menopause than they have for years." Another woman says: "Since I have had my menopause, I have felt like a teen-ager again. I can remember my mother saying that after her menopause she really got her vigor, and I can say the same thing about myself. I'm just never tired now."

In another study, 21 percent of the women in the age group between fifty-five and sixty-five felt that "after menopause a woman is more interested in sex than before." A doctor who said these findings agreed with his clinical experience added: "Many younger women come into the office complaining of minor menstrual irregularities or pre-menstrual tension, but seriously concerned that they may be having signs of menopause. However, when the actual time arrives the older woman is quite ready to accept it, with perhaps a few tears and slight depression, but on the whole well pleased with her lack of symptoms."

As another woman said: "Perhaps it's only the middle-aged or older woman who can separate the old wives' tales from the true wives' tales."

One Ovary Is Better Than None?

"Hang on to your ovaries as long as you can ... one ovary is better than none," advises the Boston Women's Health Book Collective in *Our Bodies Ourselves.* "Ovaries produce small, but important, amounts of estrogen even after menopause. This estrogen builds bones, steadies systems, and helps in other ways."

But sometimes the uterus, tubes, and ovaries must be removed for medical reasons, perhaps because of fibroid tumors. These benign tumors, composed of fibrous tissue, attach themselves to the walls of the uterus. Fibroids are of varying sizes—from smaller than a pea to larger than a fist—and are present in varying degrees in about 30 percent of all women. Because they put pressure on other organs, they may cause irregular bleeding, prolonged menstrual periods, or massive hemmorrhages. If so, and depending upon location of the fibroid, surgeons may remove (hysterectomy) uterine fibroids without interfering with uterine function; they may remove the body of the uterus but not of the cervix (this is the *simple hysterectomy* most women go through); or perform total hysterectomy plus removal of ovaries and tubes (*radical hysterectomy*). Doctors can also perform a *myomectomy* which removes only the tumor, leaving the uterus intact.

Dr. Harold T. Hyman, in his *Complete Home Medical Encyclopedia* writes: "Note ... that ovarian function and secretions are unimpaired after simple and total hysterectomy; and that preservation of a small fragment of one ovary suffices to prevent artificial menopause after radical hysterectomy. Hence, none of these procedures adversely affects the woman's appearance or her sexual life; and none necessarily requires postoperative administration of hormones."

A certain amount of hormone is needed for sexual response, but this hormone is probably produced not in the ovaries but in the adrenal glands, which continue to function after the ovaries stop and may even step up their production to make up for the slackening of the ovaries.

Recent reports indicate that many hysterectomies may not be necessary. One doctor suggests that only one-third of all hysterectomies are justified, many others just keep the fees rolling in. The woman who trusts and respects her gynecologist should accept his or her advice. If you are in doubt, you should get another medical opinion.

Emotional Aspects Can Set the Stage for Depression

Consider the stage on which this scene is played, what has happened in previous acts ... and what the audience expects ...

Too many times, expectation leads to fact. Do we *expect* to grow older in the image of the folklore? Advertisements have taught us to picture the menopausal woman as afflicted, haggard, unstable, tired, irritable, depressed, unsexy, and unattractive. (Who wants to "grow gracefully" into *that*!)

Like most stereotypes, the image distorts, although it's true that emotional ups and downs influence the menopausal years. Nevertheless, depression is the most frequently diagnosed malady in outpatient clinics today, according to Dr. Leopold Bellak, a noted New York psychiatrist. Dr. Bellak believes that depression is usually a reaction to feeling helpless.

Often women arrive at the time of menopause with a sense of imminent defeat and impending loneliness. They fear they will lose their youthful looks, their children, and their major social role—as mother—all in the same period of life.

Dr. Estelle Ramey, writing in *Johns Hopkins Magazine*, describes the woman whose husband is probably going to die before she does. "She is a wonderful wife and mother. She has a B.A. from Radcliffe, magna cum laude in Sanskrit, and this makes her a superb mother. She does all the things she is supposed to. She does them well, and she is happy as a lark, sometimes. She is a little bored, but she may not even be aware of it.

"She gets to the watershed age of 50, at which point several things may happen. First of all, a catastrophe has occurred in the family. The kids have grown up. She has given them her life and they want only their own lives. They leave. It is very hard to bear. She is menopausal. When she was young she had raging hormones, and who wanted her in a tough job of top responsibility with raging hormones? Then her hormones stopped raging and she is a menopausal woman. Who wants a menopausal woman around? Certainly not her 50-year-old husband. He wants someone closer to his own age, say, 21."

One depression-causing feeling of helplessness comes from realizing that society hasn't truly recognized women as valuable members, except in the child-rearing role. "Buck up, sweetie, we'll go to Florida," may perk a woman up a bit, but it doesn't replace a lifelong sense of meaning that is now in a state of transition, along with the hormones.

We all know mild depressions in times of stress or helplessness. Dr. John O'Connor suggests that for some women menopause triggers true depression (involutional depression) signaled by sadness, hypochondriasis, impairment of concentration . . . later guilt, worthlessness, psychomotor retardation, fear, agitation. Dr. O'Connor says that the most common factors precipitating involutional depression at this age are: (1) the independence and departure from home of the children; (2) death of parents and friends; (3) an increased tendency toward illness; and (4) decreased potency of the husband.

A woman's early environment, personality development, and current life status may contribute to depression. The woman who has always been reared to be "ladylike," compliant, a "good wife" and "good mother" may become depressed because she isn't emotionally flexible. When "a change" occurs, whether physiological, psychological, or environmental—such women may not be able to compensate or adjust. Yet, Dr. O'Connor sees a falling off of serious depression among middle-aged women, and he attributes the decline to antidepressants and the fact that more women are working and developing interests outside the home. "It is probable, too," he adds, "that the increasing awareness of women of their own sexuality and the greater freedom permitted in expressing it have contributed to the decline of these cases."

How Can You "Cure" The Symptoms?

If you are a woman, you can help yourself diminish the effects of menopausal hot flashes, vaginal atrophy, moodiness, and weight gains. Those around you—husband, children, friends—can help, too. Each woman should, with the help of her doctor, research the possibilities in estrogen, exercise, new eating habits, and "outreach."

Estrogen, the female hormone responsible for secondary sex characteristics, declines with age, causing various symptoms. Estrogen losses accompanying menopause affect the metabolic, sensory, digestive, skeletal, glandular, muscular, vasomotor, cardiovascular, and central nervous systems. You may not feel the effects directly, but the work of these systems is tied to the estrogen in the body. Sometimes a doctor will analyze a woman's medical background and hormonal needs and decide to replace some of the lost estrogen. Estrogen-replacement therapy means giving doses of natural or synthetic estrogen to compensate for loss. Estrogen comes in a natural form (Premarin) or in synthetic forms (Meprane, Progynon, Stilbestrol). Stilbestrol, however, is being questioned as a possible cancer-causing agent.

Most recent medical reports say that hot flashes and genital atrophy are the only "uniquely characteristic" menopausal symptoms. These, too, are the only symptoms uniformly relieved by estrogen therapy. Estrogen therapy will *not* properly treat insomnia, irritability, depression, nausea, or sagging sex life. Masters and Johnson said of older women " . . . elevation of sexual responsiveness rarely results directly from the administration of estrogen or estrogen-like products." It is important, in other words, to take estrogen for the "right reason."

A Maturation Index, or microscopic examination of vaginal cells, can determine a woman's estrogen needs. Doctors say that women with a history of breast or uterine cancer or kidney, liver, or heart disease should *not* be treated with estrogen.

With or without estrogen-replacement therapy, a woman's body will continue to produce small amounts of estrogen well into her late years. Women need a certain amount of estrogen for building body tissues and for holding nitrogen in the cells. Without enough nitrogen, muscle cells lose their strength, and bones become brittle.

Although estrogen may relieve hot flashes and create a feeling of well-being, doctors agree that, at the present time, it must not be extolled as an "old-age panacea." Medical specialists are still concerned with possible cancer and heart-disease complications. Future research must validate estrogen-replacement therapy to alleviate psychic, sexual, and behavioral discomforts associated with menopause.

Diet and Exercise Can Play Their Part

In some senses, we are what we eat. Since some women gain weight during menopause, you should be more careful of your diet. During and after menopause a diet high in protein and low in carbohydrates may maximize energy and control weight. In addition to a well-balanced diet, women should get plenty of liquids and roughage to aid regularity and well-being.

Consider these examples of ways of adjusting to the menopause:

• A Peace Corps nurse in Malaysia (herself a beautiful sixty-five) writes that she stays trim and vigorous with hard work, good diet, and daily doses of Vitamin C. About Malaysian women and menopause she says: "Women who work very hard don't have time for minor sufferings . . . or identity crises."

• "Sex, biking, and ballet," are one fifty-year-old woman's answer to her exercise needs. "When my exercise level drops, so do my moods. I can condition the way I feel by what I do. In a stress period, such as menopause, I exercise more. It doesn't *cure* all symptoms, but it certainly helps me weather them satisfactorily."

• And a sporting outfitter in New York offers a special new bicycle—a three-wheeler built for two (adults!). A rear basket holds at least a week's groceries—and a sign dangles from the striped canopy, "Don't let an energy crisis get *you*!"

Whether it's vitamins and vegetables or yogurt and yoga, female systems in transition profit from well-planned diet and exercise. Reaching out to the world—searching for new projects, work, involvements and relationships, and new risks—can "cure" boredom, loneliness, moodiness, and fatigue. A husband's expressions of caring make the real difference for women in times of stress or transition.

How a Husband Can Help

A noted gerontologist suggests that a husband can help his wife through this period if he is especially considerate. For example, he can take care to show her that she is appreciated and still attractive. He can pamper her and show his interest by remembering anniversaries and birthdays and by taking her out more often. Instead of crouching behind a newspaper or watching television in the evening, he can talk to his wife and show an interest in what she's doing and thinking. When one's wife is in a bad humor or moody and depressed, sympathize with her moods and remain tolerant. Invite her out for an evening's entertainment, or plan a trip to take together.

A middle-aged man in Alabama wrote a letter to the New York *Times* to tell of *his* feelings about his wife's fortieth birthday. He said that after some years of taking her for granted, it one day occurred to him "unexpectedly, delightfully" that he was married to a grown, mature, exciting woman. "I began to sing. I laughed. I whooped. I realized with a thrill that I had fallen in love again," he said. No woman could feel too dispirited about aging while eliciting responses like that. The husband concluded, "It takes forty years to build into a woman that depth, glamour, and mystery which make up the vital ingredient of human delight: spirit."

Is There Sex After Menopause?

Menopause doesn't end sex—unless you want it to. But some women feel that their sexual life is over when their reproductive capacity wanes. Some couples who never had a very satisfactory sex life welcome menopause as an excuse to stop sexual relations.

Actually, woman's sexual life after menopause is a puzzle: the capacity for sexual response remains the same and desire usually increases; however, the frequency of intercourse declines.

A woman's sex life usually tapers off because a man's sexual interest declines. Yet the woman's interest remains steady or increases until very late years. A woman improves with age . . . particularly when she is regularly exposed to effective sexual stimulation.

The Duke University studies (Chapter IV) revealed that women cease sexual relations because the husband becomes ill or impotent, or dies. The menopause and the decade after should be a time of "best sex ever" if a woman's responses have been cultivated and a man's desire continues. Sexual communication from her husband (or partner) counteracts a woman's doubts about her general worthiness or attractiveness. One psychologist says: "The menopause might even bring a couple closer together. If each can share what the experience means to them, they might understand and grow. If they keep their feelings to themselves—it can lead to withdrawal and alienation."

When a woman has a partner, maintaining sexual activity into old age depends, most importantly, on regular sexual expression in the earlier years. One woman writer suggests that perhaps the next generation of women, freer to express their sexuality and individuality in their younger years, will prolong their own sexual activity and also their partners'.

How to Cope with the Realities

Sex organs deteriorate with age largely because of hormonal changes. Vaginal linings may be dry, muscles loose, lubrication scanty. But modern science offers jellies, creams, therapeutic exercises, estrogen-replacement therapy, and surgery for specific instances.

Kegel exercises help many women build up their pelvic muscles, which have been stretched and weakened by childbirth. These exercises can increase a woman's ability to satisfy her husband and can teach her voluntary control. (See Chapter IX for a fuller explanation.)

Occasionally, Kegel exercises fail to build up the muscles sufficiently. Then a doctor may consider vaginoplasty, vaginal plastic surgery. This operation repairs torn ligaments and muscles and, possibly, removes stretched or excess tissues.

Some physical changes may occur in the postmenopausal years, including loss of subcutaneous (beneath the skin) fat, wrinkling of the skin, a loss of substance to and sagging of the breasts, and thickening of the midriff and other areas. Post menopausal women may also be prone to cystitis, an infection and inflammation of the bladder. But these and other problems can respond to medical treatment and the right social and psychological environment, in which the woman, her doctor, and those close to her lend physical and mental support.

Most doctors say that a woman is *not* more prone to develop cancer at the menopause. Most cancer of the womb occurs before menopause, and cancer of the body of the womb follows it, usually over a period of years.

In short, the postmenopausal years should be filled with good health and good sex ... free of what one woman called "those damn periods" and the fear of pregnancy. After menstruation has stopped for one year, a woman isn't likely to become pregnant, although birth control measures should be continued for another six months; women over forty are most likely to bear mongoloid or deformed children.

Outlets for Widows

Most women end up as widows. Women outlive men (possibly their natural estrogen protects them from heart disease), but they have fewer chances for remarriage. More than ten million widows live in America, where social, legal, and economic customs still regard them as possessions of their husbands. Widows say that it's difficult to get charge accounts, mortgages, jobs—let alone another husband!

In the older age groups, unattached men are free to marry (or date) a full field of older women or to select a new younger partner. Older women are not so free to meet or choose younger men. Most remain unmarried—to cope with grief, finances, future crises, and the various frustrations of being alone.

Counseling services for widows are being developed. The Widows Consultation Center in New York City helps widows figure out everything from "pounding a nail in the wall to managing insurance money." Their address is 136 East 57th St., New York, N.Y. 10022.

Money aside, most widows agree that sorting out their feelings about remarriage presents the greatest conflicts. The widows' agencies offer people a chance to talk to other widows who have confronted the same feelings. A group called Widow to-Widow is funded by the National Institute of Mental Health and headed by Dr. Phyllis R. Silverman, lecturer in social welfare, Department of Psychiatry, Harvard Medical School. Widows, Inc., in Houston, Texas, is another consultation service created to help widows (or widowers) meet practical problems satisfactorily. The Information Center for Mature Women (515 Madison Ave., New York, N.Y. 10022) can provide much helpful information for older women—whether married, widowed, or single.

Another personal problem faces the woman who had an active satisfying sex life until the death of her husband: how does she handle her sex drives? A financial adviser is easy enough to find—but who will talk about sex? Usually no one speaks of sex (to widows) and few acknowledge the intense need—so she sweeps the ideas under the . . . bed.

Alfred Kinsey found that sustained interest in sex continues longer than sexual activity. In other words, older people (especially those who are unmarried) are much more apt to think or fantasize about sexual affairs than they are to have them. But the interest lives.

Along this line, Kinsey's work provided some raw data in the field of sex research, but it omitted exploration of the emotional aspects of sexual relationships. Just as love takes many forms (sex is but one), sex has many expressions.

The contemporary philosopher Dr. Duncan Littlefair says: "It is shocking to me, always, to have intimacy be equated with sex. And it is a shocking revelation and indication of our day that the two words are almost invariably related. I have noticed when I have said that I am intimate with her or him that there is a slight raising of eyebrows. I have noticed in conversations that when you say two people are intimate, that the assumption is that they sleep together. This is a degradation of the spirit, for intimacy is much, much more important than sex, and indeed without intimacy, sex is nothing. And since sex is so nothing for so many, we must assume that intimacy plays very little part in it. And it is possible for people to be sexually interdependent and have no intimacy at all, for there is something more than the body with which to relate to other people."

Without making judgments about the emotional quality, it's probable that marital and extramarital sex satisfy some. Lesbianism, fantasies, or masturbation please others.

But certain women don't want to practice lesbianism or masturbation—need or no need! They rechannel much basic sexual energy (libido) in nonsexual activites that may expend energy and give some pleasure. People do satisfy themselves in golf, tennis, politics, careers, hobbies, television, dirty movies, and social causes.

A group of elderly people have established a political party, the Grey Panthers, to work through political channels to create a more "liberated" and just environment for older people.

Yet warns Dr. Masters, "Deprived of normal sexual outlets women exhaust themselves physically in conscious and unconscious efforts to dissipate their accumulated sexual tensions. They cast themselves into religion, the business world, volunteer social work, overzealous mothering of mature children or grandchildren."

However, many physical and emotional outlets are perfectly

acceptable. For many persons, kind words and caring hands give as much pleasure as "straight sex."

"To live is to love," wrote Dr. Karl Menninger, founder of the famous mental health clinic. He meant that the only way you can live is through interdependent relationships that sustain you—and all of life. Do you suppose that the most real apprehension about change (any change—menopause, widowhood, etc.) is based on the fear that the quality of our human relationships might change or that our acceptance of those relationships (your relationship to yourself, for example) might be altered? Good sleep, nutrition, exercise, careful thought, sex, loving relationships, and medical guidance all help us to "manage aging" and to keep life evolving—at any rate and at any stage.

As part of living, menopause changes women—often for the better. Menopause can mean new beginnings in sexual freedom, a chance to face the future with new confidence and to experiment with new life-styles.

The dominant medical belief is that menopause is basically the beginning of menstruation in reverse—a return of the reproductive organs to their former quiescent state. Where problems exist, they are usually a result of negative attitudes that can be relieved by positive self-esteem. And before you think that women have *all* the problems during the menopausal years, read the next chapter about the problems *men* face during the "male menopause."

VI
NOT FOR MEN ONLY

"What happens above a man's neck is vastly more important than what happens below his belt," says Dr. William Ferber, a prominent New York urologist.

Score another point for mind over matter. It's the key to what influences a man's sexual drive, potency, and performance when he's in his "foolish forties" and "frenzied fifties."

Unfortunately, these years are the time of a man's greatest *psychological stress.* At age twenty-five he might not have known where he was going, but he knew he had lots of time to get there. At age forty-five, a man still may not know where he's going, but he's already three-quarters of the way there.

He's probably at his career plateau—trying desperately to hang on while unseen forces push him toward the brink. Even if he's reached the top, the view might not be worth the climb.

His interests are narrowing and his options are fewer. He's not going to change jobs, wives, or social position. He's more set in his ways, clinging to familiar patterns, people, and places. He's inflating the past—not committing himself to the future.

One middle-aged executive told me: "I'm forty-seven and hoped I was in line for a vice-presidency. Then they appointed a thirty-four-year-old kid to the job who talks a jargon I can't understand. His ideas are fresh and bright; he dismisses my suggestions as 'old hat.' Then I walk down the street and meet a pretty girl. I give her a first glance . . . then a second. She doesn't even look my way!"

Another man described middle age as a "nowhere time of life." He said you look ahead and see a lot of tottering old people . . . you look back and see a generation of young people who have "turned you off and tuned you out."

Add to these men's burdens the psychological and financial handicaps of sending kids to college, fighting to keep ahead of inflation, and the fact that his marriage might be going "stale," and you've got a man on an emotional merry-go-round.

Instead of his life resting on a bedrock of power, success, and financial security, our hero is sinking in a quicksand of doubt. As another man confided: "I haven't the time, but I understand the men who drink too much and play around with other women; at least these options are still open."

Dr. Willard Gaylin, Manhattan psychiatrist, says: "Middle-class men whose lives are oriented to work, status, achievement sometimes turn to sexual activity for reassurance. Having gone as far as they can go, they try to find in sex what they can no longer find at the marketplace, and at the same time, blind themselves to the idea of encroaching age."

Sex does become the whipping post of many a man who is frustrated in his job and home life. His wife, who has physical and psychological problems of her own (as discussed in the previous chapter), adds to the burdens and complaints. And as the children leave home and the job holds less promise, husband and wife have fewer bonds in common and fewer commitments to each other.

Some men compensate by stepping up their marital sex life. One wife of a fifty-five-year-old executive said that her husband insisted on having sex every night just to prove he "was still as good as he once was."

Other men turn to extramarital affairs to stimulate their sexual lives. Unfortunately, some studies confirm the effects of new and varied sex partners in stimulating activity. In one study of older rats (no pun intended), copulation more than doubled when the male had a choice of several partners.

Men who married young, who had little or no sexual experience before marriage, and who have remained faithful for years are especially vulnerable. One woman said: "The ones you have to watch out for are the ones who have been *too* good until now. Suddenly they think they may have missed something and try to make up for lost time before it's too late."

Another woman, just through the menopause, was dismayed to find that her husband wanted a divorce to marry a younger woman— because he wanted more children! As one man quipped: "I don't mind being a grandfather, but I can't stand being married to a grandmother."

A man's "delayed adolescence" may take the form of playing the "numbers game"—trying to maintain or reach the "average" number of sexual contacts per week (or month). What these men overlook is that there's no real "average": one man's sex habits may seem like debauchery to another and almost abstinence to a third. One doctor told me: "There's no such thing as an average. A man should have sex when—and only when—he really wants and needs it. If middle-aged men would relax and have sex only at those times, they could keep on indefinitely."

As Dr. A.L. Wolbarst wrote in the *New York State Journal of Medicine*: "We can test a man for his hearing, digestive powers, his fertility . . . but not for his sexual powers." And a noted sexologist, Dr. Wilhelm Stekel, believes that a man becomes old only when he feels old . . . he becomes impotent only when he gives up his potency. He adds: "In men the capacity for erection begins on the day of birth and extinguishes with death."

Most men should take comfort in the Kinsey studies that showed that the rate at which males slow up sexually in later years is no different than the rate at which they slow up in earlier years. The studies found there was no point at which old age entered the picture. The oldest person in their studies was an eighty-eight-year-old man married to (and still sexually active with) a ninety-year-old wife. And one man of seventy was ejaculating seven times a week.

If men think they have a problem, it would help if they could confide in a friend (or a sympathetic doctor). But men usually hide their anxieties in locker-room jokes rather than in frank confidences. In *The Wonderful Crisis of Middle Age*, Eda J. LeShan points out that while women can hug, and kiss, and exchange confidences, men are less flexible emotionally. They seldom have a real "pal" to whom they can unburden themselves. This emotional isolation from other men places an extra burden—and a barrier—on a man who needs psychological relief.

What Are Some Male Psychological Symptoms?

Between the ages of forty-five and sixty, most men experience increases in one or more of these symptoms: nervousness, decrease or loss of sexual potential, depression, decreased memory and concentration, decreased or absent sex drive, fatigue, sleeplessness, irritability, loss of interest and self-confidence, indecisiveness, numbness and tingling, fear of impending danger, excitability, constipation, crying, hot flashes, chills, itching, sweating, cold hands and feet . . .

Dr. August A. Werner, of the St. Louis University School of Medicine, listed thirty-five symptoms that men and women go through during this stage (when the woman is going through her change of life) and found only minor differences between the sexes.

But although a woman *knows* the physical causes for her psychological problems, a man can't trace a cause and effect. It's no comfort to heed the words of Dr. Charles Wahl, a psychiatrist at the University of California (Los Angeles): "These symptoms are of a psychic origin when found in a man who is not afflicted by a specific disease. The body undergoes no organic or functional changes that might account for such complaints."

But testosterone (male hormone) levels go down when stress levels go up, and the first part of a man's makeup to suffer is his sex drive. This fact was borne out in studies of combat soldiers, in which sex ranked *twentieth* in a list of urgent desires—behind a furlough, good food, and clean sheets. Army sexual athletes were usually rear-echelon soldiers. When *Time* magazine reported the liberation of Paris and told of jeeps parked outside apartment houses all night and tousled girls climbing out of tanks, the item failed to mention that these troops had seen little or no combat; the combat troops were too busy drinking or reminiscing even to consider sex.

Just as war can take away a man's sex drive, war with himself has the same effect. Thus, a man under stress must reduce or relieve the stress before he can regain his libido. But many men react to stress by adding more stressful situations. A man may react to the fear of losing his job by working harder. A man concerned with his sex drive may increase the sexual demands on both his mind and body; he may concentrate so hard on the "demands" of foreplay that he rushes through it to an incomplete or premature ejaculation —causing even more stress.

Dr. Hans Selye, University of Montreal, suggests that a man should seek the best alternative for each form of stress. His simple formula: if there's too much stress on any one part, you need *diversion*; if there's too much on the whole, you need *rest*.

Diversion means a change of pace or scene. If you feel "keyed up," try doing something else for a change. You might simply go to the movies, read a book, or visit a friend. Or you might work off your steam by gardening, walking, sports. Either way, you'll relax taut nerves, tensed muscles, wrought-up glands ... you'll feel re-freshed and ready to tackle the situation anew.

Don't wait until you're about to "explode"; you might do something rash that increases tension. Diversion can prevent ex-plosions; one study of persons hospitalized because of mental disorders showed that 57 percent had no planned recreational or crea-tive activities during the year prior to hospitalization. In contrast, only 10 percent of well-adjusted subjects had no purposeful ac-tivities.

Rest can ease stress because human beings, like automobile tires, last longer when they wear evenly over a long period of time. Unfortunately, when you're under stress you may find it harder to calm down and get the rest or sleep you need. But if you go away for a restful week or weekend, you'll probably unwind enough to rest or sleep.

Avoid eating too much when you're under stress; you can't digest as well if your stomach is "all churned up." And while a little tension or stress helps increase sexual excitement, too much tension hinders sex.

Just as a husband can help his wife through the menopause (see the previous chapter), so can a wife help her husband. The thought-ful wife can bolster her husband's ego by being aware of what deflates him and what builds him up. Concentrate on building up his self-confidence, and avoid nagging criticisms and arguments. Show your husband how much you need him and depend upon him; sustain his sense of self-importance. Be affectionate and give him tender, loving care, especially if you feel that he is worried or tense. He may want more company than usual or he may prefer not to go out socially. Whatever the case, give in to him. He'll resume his normal pace after a while.

Is There a Physical Basis for "Male Menopause?"

From a biological standpoint a man's hormonal levels may decline, but there aren't enough endocrine changes to account for physical symptoms—except for possible loss of energy.

From another viewpoint, a man doesn't go through a "change of life" as does a women, simply because he still remains capable (in most cases) of siring children. Even if the testicles gradually reduce spermatozoa production in a man's fifties, he is still capable of fathering children well into his sixties, seventies, and even eighties.

Psychiatrist Helen Kaplan, director of the Paine-Whitney Sex-Therapy Clinic, Cornell Medical School, says: "If the definition is an abrupt, age-related change in the reproductive biology then there is no male climacteric. If the definition is a psychophysiological con-stellation that occurs in our culture in some men—then there is. The psychological symptoms are a reaction to the physiological symptoms."

There are physical changes that can be measured. With advancing years, the testicles become less firm and actually reduce in size. The ejaculatory jets gradually weaken, and the ejaculate becomes scantier. The output of testosterone (male sex hormone) declines gradually, though slowly, in most men until they reach age sixty, after which it remains relatively constant.

Dr. Barry M. Segal, endocrinologist of Phelps Memorial Hospital, Tarrytown, New York, says: "In men, changes occur in middle age because of their changing levels of hormone distribution. Although their hormone levels decrease as they age, men never stop functioning and continue manufacturing hormones all their lives. The responsive level is never totally absent and men have been known to be fertile well past age 70."

Although a man's testicles may be physically capable of producing sperm and hormones, they may stop their production for other than purely physical reasons. The decline may be due to stress or emotional upset of the system, which causes the "instructions" (pituitary secretions that stimulate hormonal production) to become skewered or lost. But this would be a *psychological* rather than physical reason for declining hormonal production. The only purely physical reason—when the testes fail to obey instruction because they are too old or tired—is called "primary testicular insufficiency."

Says Dr. Herbert S. Kupperman, associate professor of medicine at New York University Medical Center: "A man who is in acute or chronic stress, which may cause a testosterone deficiency, which may cause impaired sexual performance, which may cause depression is not a man in the climacteric—he's a depressed man."

Outside stresses and faulty body chemistry can produce depressed states—apathy and loss of self-esteem, appetite, and sexual drive. The victim may have moods that swing from morning "highs" to evening "lows." Depression can also run in families.

Earlier family trauma often sows the seeds of depression. Let's take the case of a successful businessman, Jonathan C., who thought he was a "failure." His love life had shriveled, he shunned parties and socializing, and he felt he was through at age fifty-four. He had made appointments with a psychiatrist on the insistence of his wife, who couldn't understand why Jonathan didn't want to make love.

In probing into Jonathan's background, the psychiatrist found that Jonathan's father was a perfectionist who demanded equally high standards in his son. Jonathan loved his pretty mother and was affectionate toward her, but she always sided with his father whenever the older man criticized his son.

When Jonathan married and he and his wife visited his parents, the father continued criticizing the son, although Jonathan had made a mark in the business father had suggested. Jonathan's mother, as usual, would agree with the father, and Jonathan felt again like a guilty, inferior little boy.

On his father's death, Jonathan succeeded to the presidency of his firm, but his mother damned his achievements with faint praise, while lauding the virtues of his late father. No matter what Jonathan did to prove his success, it wasn't good enough for the mother—nor did it compare with his father's successes.

When his mother died, Jonathan plunged into deep gloom. He thought his grief stemmed from his sense of personal loss, but under psychiatric care, he came to realize that his grief was more complex. Basically, he had competed with his father for his mother's love. Even when he found a satisfactory mate and had proven himself in the business world, he was still competing. His mother's death removed his last chance to "win" or take her away from the father. By realizing these conflicts, Jonathan was able to face life realistically, count his blessings, and appreciate his wife more. His love life improved, and his depression evaporated.

Not all depressions have earlier roots. Many depressions stem directly from anxieties caused during these middle and later years, and symptoms range from mild to very severe. Both men and women may become preoccupied with their bodies and experience delusions about their lives.

It's not uncommon for menopausal men and women to want to "call it quits." They feel they've been "good" all these years, and they aren't being rewarded for their good behavior. Sometimes they feel rejected by spouse, employers, and friends, and they turn this rejection into self-hate. The result can be anything from a sore throat to a suicide attempt.

Some men feel if they can just "hang on" everything will be all right eventually. But Dr. Daniel J. Levinson, Yale University psychologist, feels that you should use this unsettled period to try for something new. He explains: "There's more possibility here than just survival. If you try for big changes, you may fail miserably. On the other hand, if you don't try for big changes, you'll feel dead in a few years because you'll be stagnant."

The menopausal years *can* be the best years of your life. The kids should be grown or taken care of, you should have acquired most everything you need or want, and you should be freer to do *what you want*—when you want to do it. You're still in the driver's seat in business and in government. Instead of letting people tell you where to go, now's the time to tell them where to get off.

Many people can relieve transitory depression by *shifting gears fast*—thinking or doing something else. When this doesn't work, your doctor can treat some forms of depression with drugs, including lithium carbonate. In other cases, doctors may recommend psychotherapy or electric-shock therapy, which often helps.

If a man's problem is primarily sexual, adding (administering) male hormones helps only when a deficiency exists. But any improvement may stem more from a placebo effect of the hormone, or the fact that it might generally improve a person's physical and mental well-being.

Adds Dr. Kupperman: "If you take a hundred impotent men and treat them with testosterone, 18 percent will respond. But if you do tests and treat only those with a hormonal deficiency, you'll get a 90 percent response. When a man is impotent with his wife but doing well with other women, there's no climacteric. When a man says he can't get erections with women but wakes up with spontaneous erections—that man has no true climacteric. It's all in the head." (We'll discuss impotence in greater detail in the next chapter).

Since testicular failure can occur at any age, and because it's an illness like diabetes or kidney trouble, any man who suspects he might have this physical problem should see his doctor. Hormones *might* help, but hormones can also be dangerous, as they could contribute to cancer of the prostate.

Problems With the Prostate

The prostate doesn't do a heck of a lot, but it sure can kick up a fuss. It's a rubbery mass of glands and muscle tissue shaped roughly like a horse chestnut, and situated immediately beneath the bladder. It surrounds the urethra (the canal through which the urine is discharged) and the ejaculatory jets.

The main function of the prostate is to supply the milky fluid that nourishes and transports the semen. Up to about age fifty, the prostate gland doesn't give its owner much trouble, but after that age, it can start kicking up.

Before age fifty most prostate trouble is caused by bacterial or viral-like infections, including gonorrhea. Prostate trouble can also be caused by sexual irregularity. The gland is constantly secreting a certain amount of fluid, and it doubles or triples this amount when a person is sexually aroused.

Like any other organ, the prostate gets used to—and is prepared to respond to—a certain amount of activity. If it's regularly called upon to supply so much fluid for so many ejaculations per week or month, it will function accordingly. But if the owner abstains or cuts back, the prostate is like a merchant who has stocked his warehouse in anticipation of a certain amount of business. If business falls off, his economic health falters and his merchandise spoils. If he gets a "run" or panic buying, the prostate (merchant) may soon find himself without anything to supply (sell).

Prostate trouble may also be caused by *coitus interruptus* (in which the man withdraws before ejaculating). In this process, the man may not completely ejaculate all the secretion and not adequately empty the prostate. Thus, it may become congested and inflamed.

Although venereal infection and irregular sexual habits may cause prostatitis (prostate trouble), no man should look upon it as anything to be ashamed of or as a sign that something is wrong with his sex life.

Some medical authorities feel that lack of zinc in the diet may cause prostate enlargement, and they recommend eating zinc-rich foods like brewer's yeast, nuts, molasses, eggs, rice bran, onions, rabbit, chicken, peas, beans, lentils, wheat germ and bran, beef liver, and gelatin.

After age fifty, the prostate may become inflamed or enlarged as part of the normal aging process. According to researchers, by age sixty, six out of ten men have an enlarged prostate, and by age seventy, almost all men have this problem.

As the prostate surrounds the urethra and ejaculatory jets, you can imagine that the first sign of trouble may by difficulty in urinating or in ejaculating.

The enlarged gland can narrow the urinary canal, making it difficult to urinate. It can cause pain or bleeding in urination, and the stream may narrow and lack force. Because the bladder can't empty properly, a man may feel that he needs to urinate more often.

When a man gets an erection or ejaculates, an enlarged prostate can cause pain and even premature ejaculation.

A person with prostate trouble can also have referred pain in the lower abdomen, thighs, and rectal area. His rectum may feel full, but having a bowel movement fails to relieve the pressure. He may also have chills, fever, and general bodily discomfort.

If you have any of these symptoms, see your doctor. The doctor can tell a lot about your prostate by a simple rectal examination, which can reveal any enlargement, inflammation, or growth.

The doctor also learns much from a patient's case history, by determining problems or difficulties in urinating, by chemically analyzing the urine, by taking blood tests and X rays, and by various probes and biopsy. Often the simple rectal examination will do. That's why it is so important for men over age forty to have a rectal examination at regular intervals. If your doctor detects a diseased or enlarged prostate early, the chances are that he can cure it completely. But if he detects it too late, the condition might be fatal.

For example, let's take the case of a fifty-three-year-old man who has just had a rectal examination. The doctor has found a nodule—a knoblike growth—in the prostate.

This nodule is small, localized, and probably benign. But if it were allowed to remain, or if it turned out to be cancerous, it could spread rapidly and destroy the patient. Thus, a simple operation now—removal of the nodule—could prevent a cancerous growth.

Even a simple enlarged prostate causes problems. If the bladder cannot be emptied completely, infection can result. Such an infection may not only affect the prostate and bladder, but it might spread upward to infect the kidneys.

Another reason for early detection is that symptoms aren't always in proportion to enlargement. A very slight enlargement may completely obstruct the flow of urine; a large inflammation may cause few, if any, symptoms.

Doctors treat most cases of prostatitis with antibiotics or by prostate massage. A therapist massages the prostate by inserting a finger into the rectum and pressing rhythmically against the gland. If the prostate is congested, massage will empty it of debris and pus.

If antibiotics and massage don't work, the therapist can try other remedies, including hot baths, diets that avoid spicy foods and alcohol, and treatment with antihistimine and antitrichomonas drugs, even tranquilizers. Perhaps ninety-nine out of one hundred cases of prostatitis will respond to the above treatments, but there are times when the doctor must consider surgery.

Most enlarged prostates are classified as benign growths. Like all benign growths, they wreak their damage by taking up space and putting pressure on surrounding tissues—usually the urethra in the case of an enlarged prostate.

About the only sure way to cure a benign growth is to remove all or part of it. But, in the case of the prostate, if the growth is developing slowly and is not blocking the urine, the doctor may decide (especially if the patient is in his sixties or seventies) to ignore the swelling, assuming that the patient will die of other causes before the prostate enlargement causes trouble.

If the growth is cancerous, the doctor almost invariably must operate, as the disease will spread rapidly, sometimes shortly causing death.

Cancer of the prostate rarely appears in men under age forty, but after age fifty-five it becomes the third-highest site of cancer among men, and after age seventy-five the main site. The first major symptom of prostate cancer is pain in the pelvis, lower back, or upper thighs. Other symptoms may be similar to those of benign prostate growth, and the cancer may develop in connection with a benign tumor.

Doctors cure or arrest prostate cancer by surgery (described below), by orchiectomy (surgical removal of the testicles), and/or by estrogen therapy (the male hormone may be partly responsible for prostate cancer; the female hormone combats this tendency). However, hormone therapy also may increase the possibility of death from heart disease, blood-vessel disease, or stroke.

Surgery of the Prostate

If your doctor decides to operate (prostatectomy), he may remove part or all of the prostate. Or he may perform a preliminary operation, called a cystostomy, to relieve and drain the bladder before performing the prostatectomy.

In cystostomy, the doctor makes an incision in the center of the lower abdomen, midway between the navel and the pubic bone. He inserts a needlelike tube into the bladder to drain the contents.

To operate on the prostate, the physician approaches it in one of several ways: (1) over the pubic bone and into the bladder; (2) under the public bone without opening the bladder; (3) through the floorlike surface separating the scrotum and the anus; or (4) through the urethra (urine canal).

This last approach, called *transurethra prostatectomy*, uses a slender tube that slips into the urinary channel and into the bladder. This sophisticated instrument has an electric light at its far end and contains a series of lenses that permit the surgeon to view the various organs. The surgeon does the cutting with a wirelike electric knife. This knife shaves away slices of tissue, while the electric currrent cauterizes the area, keeping bleeding to a minimum. The surgeon continues cutting until he has removed all foreign tissue.

Doctors prefer transurethral prostatectomy because it doesn't actually open the body, but it is difficult to perform and works only when the tumor is detected in an early stage. Once a malignant or benign tumor reaches a certain size, it's too big to be whittled away. That's why, again, it is so important to catch tumors at an early stage.

A relatively recent development is cryosurgery—destruction of an organ by freezing rather than cutting away. Prostatic cryosurgery involves inserting into the bladder a probe containing a liquid nitrogen system and a heating coil. The nitrogen freezes the tissue and destroys it, while the heating coil thaws the area enough to permit the probe to be extracted.

Does Prostate Surgery Cause Complications?

Prostate surgery is no more dangerous than other types of abdominal surgery. However, the patient cannot simply walk out of the hospital in a few days and feel as good as new.

"Will prostate surgery affect my sex life?" ask many patients. One doctor said it brings to mind the old story about the boy who broke his arm playing high school football. "Will I be able to play the piano when this heals?" he asked the coach. "Of course," the coach replied. "Gee, that's great," said the boy, "I never could play the piano before!"

Prostate surgery can even improve a patient's sex life if the prostatitis had caused painful erection and ejaculation. But it can cause some complications.

For instance, the physician might sever some of the nerves responsible for erection, but these nerves should grow back together shortly.

If the prostate has been completely removed, the patient can continue to ejaculate, but the ejaculate goes back into the bladder rather than forward through the urinary canal. The semen remains in the bladder until the next time the man urinates. This "retrograde ejaculation" isn't harmful and creates a problem only when a patient can't cope with it psychologically or when he still wants to sire children.

Do Women Have Prostate Problems?

As we've discussed before, the male and female sex organs (penis and clitoris; testicles and ovaries) are remarkably similar—especially in cell and tissue structure. So it is not surprising that the female has tissues and glands similar to the male prostate. Female "prostate glands," are called "Skene's glands," and they can develop diseases similar to male prostatic disorders.

Skene's glands may become inflamed, but they rarely develop benign or cancerous tumors. Gonorrhea and other infections are the main cause of trouble in Skene's glands and the urethra.

Female prostatitis symptoms are similar to those of the male: difficulty or urgency in urination, blood in the urine, vaginal discharge. Treatment usually consists of antibiotics and hot baths. If the urethra is blocked or otherwise obstructed, doctors clear it by passing progressively larger rods through it. If the blockage is caused by a tumor outside the urethra, simple surgery usually clears up the matter.

Wives of men with prostate cancer may also develop malignancies. A study by Columbia-Presbyterian Medical Center (Houston, Tex.) found that wives had an 11 percent incidence of cancers of the breast and womb, whereas these malignancies developed in just 1 percent of wives whose husbands did not have prostate cancer. The female cancers developed at least one year after that of their husband's cancer.

Is the Prostate an Erotic Gland?

Some men report pleasurable sensations (including ejaculation) through prostate massage. One patient asked his doctor if it would be safe if he insterted a three-quarter-inch vibrator into his rectum to massage his prostate. The doctor replied:

"The vibrator will massage the prostate gland, and many males report that this produces a very pleasurable feeling. It is a safe procedure provided you learn how to do it properly."

However, the doctor cautioned that no man should try this procedure without consulting his own doctor. Prostate massage is a therapy, not a recreation, and if can be harmful if not done correctly.

Although the prostate may make contributions we don't know about, doctors say that on the basis of what is known the prostate must be judged as a poor-citizen organ that detracts more than it adds, takes more than it gives, and generally serves the body poorly in relation to the benefits it provides.

As we have seen, outside of possible prostate problems, a man *doesn't* go through a physical "change of life" as does a woman. But a man's *psychological* problems during the "male menopause" are just as acute, and he needs help to cope with his problems.

A man may also develop other problems—mainly impotency and premature ejaculation—that become problems for both himself and his partner. We shall discuss some common occurrences in the next chapter and explore solutions that apply to both male and female.

VII
FRIGIDITY, IMPOTENCY, AND
WHAT ELSE IS NEW?

A man gives love in order to get sex; a woman gives sex in order to get love. This is just one theory for the differences and conflicts between men and women.

In this chapter we shall discuss some male-female cross-purposes that may account for frigidity, impotency, premature ejaculation, ejaculation incompetency—ways in which both men and women can help each other resolve these problems. In the next chapter we shall examine some medical and physical reasons for these problems, and what can be done about them.

Our society is much to blame. In *The Wonderful Crisis of Middle Age*, Eda LeShan writes: "It was during our generation that frigidity in women declined and male impotency increased, as society challenged its males to become increasingly sensitive and responsive to women's needs. The myth of male sexual dominance ended . . . we went from one extreme to another. Rather than sex becoming a true partnership in which both persons explored and experienced new possibilities together, the burden of gratification was placed on men."

Marriage manuals exhorted men to "learn to play a woman's body like a violin." They ignored the fact that many men approach lovemaking like wrestlers, not musicians.

In *Ageless Aging* Ruth Winter says that we live in a society dominated by an insatiable need for newness—resulting in rapid obsolesence that sees no difference between products and people. In work, a man must be achievement-oriented even when he doesn't feel qualified; at home he must be "emotion-oriented" even when he doesn't feel up to it. As a result, the man doesn't know how or when to approach a woman; he takes sex when he can get it—when the woman wants to dole it out.

Another theory holds that men love with their hearts and women with their heads. And while women may have been trained to

ration their love, men haven't learned such control. What complicates
the picture is the Freudian theory that some men secretly fear and
hate their wives or partners ... fearing them because they depend
upon them; hating them for this dependency.

In a recent interview, the noted psychiatrist Dr. Theodore I.
Rubin pointed out these differences between men and women:

• Unlike women, men don't like to admit they are dependent.
However, men are dependent on fixed and predictible routines, on
admiration from others—and on their wives.

• Many men don't like women, although they need and use
them.

• Many men fear homosexuality and will not admit to soft,
weak, "feminine" feelings. Yet, Dr. Louis P. Saxe, author of *Sex and
the Mature Man*, points out that all humans are bisexual, and that no
man should feel ashamed of the female qualities he possesses.

• Men are more prone to self-hate than are women because
they have built up such great illusions about "masculine ideals" of
courage, strength, independence. They hate themselves when they
can't meet these impossible goals.

• Men may desire their wives as mistresses, but they depend
upon them as mothers. This Oedipus complex creates conflicts, especially if the male has been under the influence of a domineering
mother.

• Men are more "achievement-oriented" in sex and equate their
sexual adequacy with the number of ejaculations and orgasms they
achieve rather than the amount of affection or love they elicit.

Part of these differences and conflicts stems from the fact that a
man can't fake his sexual potency as can a woman. His erection and
ejaculation are there for all to see and experience.

Another problem is that as a little boy he was told to love his
mother, but as he grew up he was told to "break the apron strings" if
he wanted to be a man. Thus, some men may fear that if they permit themselves to become too closely involved with women and
too dependent upon them, women may take away thier masculinity (Freud called this "castration anxiety"). The fact remains
that so many men in our society have been "emasculated" that
they need a wise and passionate woman to turn them into men
again.

As we've discussed, a man is easily aroused by sight, smell,
touch, sound, suggestion. He "wants to be wanted" by the woman he
makes love to. Father Andrew Greeley, a sociologist who writes on

sexual matters, says: "... almost all American marriages would benefit greatly from more aggressive sexuality in the wife. Her aggression must of course be tender, gentle, reassuring. But it must also be firm, determined, and irresistible." Father Greeley feels this could introduce new life into an old marriage.

Sexologists point out that sexual boredom—including lack of communication and cooperation in experimenting with new techniques—is one of the major causes of sexual failure. As the English novelist Anthony Trollope said: "Men can endure pain and fear better than boredom"—an observation that has since been confirmed by space scientists, brainwashers, and bartenders.

Dr. Daniel A. Sugarman, psychologist on the staff of St. Joseph's Hospital in Paterson, New Jersey, and coauthor of *The Search for Serenity*, stresses that the emphasis on potency interferes with performance. He adds that sex, like sleep, can't be willed, and that it takes a certain amount of relaxation and confidence. He feels that a knowledgeable woman can be a major factor in creating this relaxed, confident state and offers these do's and don'ts for couples:

• *Don't* rely uncritically on the latest sex manuals, which may emphasize technique over intimacy.

• *Don't* equate potency with making money (the economically poor husband may feel he's also sexually poor).

• *Do* respond to each other's moods. A man or woman who is genuinely depressed may not admit it, but he/she will show it by fatigue, aches, pains, and loss of appetite (including sex). A truly depressed person needs understanding and sympathy as much as he/she needs professional help. Let the person talk out the problems or vent the anger rather than bottling them up inside.

• *Do* make love a mutual activity. Dr. Sugarman agrees with Father Greeley that a woman must learn to strike her own delicate balance between "taking over" and being passive. By the same token, a woman can elicit (rather than demand) satisfaction from the man in lovemaking. Lack of cooperation and communication can leave the woman as unsatisfied as the man is unhappy. Partners should learn that hugging, fondling, and massaging are meaningful in themselves—*intimacy* even more than orgasm is an essential part of sex.

• *Do* learn to laugh at failure. Practice might not even make perfect, and not every lovemaking session ends in earth-shattering orgasms. By not expecting and demanding perfection—but resolving to have "fun" come what may—a man and a woman can learn to laugh about their mishaps rather than moan over them.

The Problems with Potency, Frigidity

Frigidity in a woman equals impotency in a man. In both sexes, it's mainly an emotional rather than a physical problem. It reminds me of the time author Garson Kanin was explaining his book *A Thousand Summers* to Johnny Carson: "Age has nothing to do with sex, you know. The greatest sex organ is the brain. It's all in your head, it all comes from up there." Carson replied: "I feel like I should put my hat on."

At worst, impotency and frigidity mean a total lack of interest in sex, including a man's inability even to achieve an erection and a woman's inability to reach a climax. At its mildest, impotency in a man means that he may be able to get an erection but cannot maintain it within the woman. In a woman, it may mean disinterest or disinclination to have sexual relations.

In any event, impotency and frigidity are *male and female problems* that must be solved together. The problems can be treated only if the couple work together for their mutual satisfaction.

Most psychologists distinguish between the rare *primary impotency*, in which the male has never been able to achieve penetration and sexual gratification, and the more common *secondary impotency*, in which the failure occurred after a long period of successful sexual functioning.

Primary impotency may be caused by a "seductive mother" (one who has made sexual overtures to her son), by religious beliefs (sex is sin), by homosexual tendencies, and by traumatic initial experiences (a man may have felt degraded or belittled by a prostitute).

Secondary impotency may be caused by various problems, but *fear* is an overriding issue. This "fear of fear" phenomenon may stem from several fears that have caused several failures. Several failures in a row—whatever the cause—set up disturbing patterns and seriously undermine a man's confidence in his sexual ability. If he "knows" he's going to fail, he probably will.

In men, secondary impotency may be caused by fear of women (rejection), fear of active or latent homosexuality, fear of "net worth" (equating making money with making love), fear of the size of sex organs (many men think their sex organs are too small; women may feel their breasts are too small—or large), fear of disapproval (the emphasis on performance), fear of punishment (sex is evil), or guilt (infidelity).

Perhaps men suffer physical problems: exhaustion, lack of sleep, or abstinence (which could lead to eventual disinterest in all sex). If a man thinks that intercourse is "bad" for him, he'll soon be *unable* to have intercourse. The noted sexologist Richard von Krafft-Ebing concluded that abstinence leads to more sexual problems than debauchery (and many doctors agree).

Just as financial shocks or reverses can lead to impotency, so can emotional shocks or domestic disagreements. "Cherchez la femme" is the psychiatrists' motto as well as detectives'. Doctors point out that the female body is "nature's spark plug of male libido and potency."

Although many women continue to be highly attractive sexually in later years, some women become slovenly and sloppy in shape and form. This turns off the male, who is more affected by sensual sights than is a woman. Dr. A. L. Wolbarst found that in 46 cases of impotency husbands were repelled by these characteristics of their wives: large or sagging breasts (21), obesity (14), unseemly hair (4), loss of hair (3), and thickening of ankles or legs (4). Most of the men felt sorry for their wives, but no matter how hard they tried, they couldn't rid themselves of their inhibitions.

When the wife is at fault, some corrective measures may help. In one case, a doctor told of treating an impotent male for eight years before he discovered that the man was disgusted by his wife's large and sagging breasts. The wife then had corrective surgery on her breasts, they became more attractive, and the man's potency returned.

Although a woman may not be as affected by the sight of a man's body, she is conscious of a man's grooming, cleanliness, neat apparel, and clean shave. As one woman said to her lover: "I don't care how handsome you are if your fingernails aren't clean." A woman is also concerned with a man's manners and courtesies—all of which add to the "sexiness" of the situation.

Many psychiatrists have written about the "envies" that woman have of men and vice versa. They say a woman may envy a man's penis whereas a man may envy a woman's breasts and ability to have children—especially if he is a latent homosexual.

A man may envy what he thinks is his wife's "carefree" role of a housewife (while he's battling in the economic jungles). A woman may envy her husband's expense-account lunches while she munches peanut-butter sandwiches with the kids.

These and other "envies" can turn into hatreds that can cause frigidity or impotency—to "punish" the other party. One doctor told of a successful businessman who married an actress. They moved to the suburbs, but the wife became bored and slipped into a casual affair. Her husband found out, but at the urging of a marriage counselor (who pointed out that his preoccupation with business was partly to blame for his wife's boredom), he "forgave" his wife.

The man became increasingly occupied with business matters, more successful, and they moved up in social circles. The wife became a skilled and accomplished hostess, entertaining many demonstrative show-business people. The husband became increasingly envious of his wife's obvious good times and hostile toward her (she wasn't "repenting" for having the affair; she was enjoying too much the fruits of his labor). Finally, he became increasingly impotent, until—at age fifty-five—he was no longer able to have an erection. The husband consulted a psychiatrist, who convinced him that his impotency stemmed from an unconscious desire to "punish" his wife (she took his sexual desire as a sign of his loving approval). The wife also went through psychotherapy, and she learned to curb her social ebullience and to be more understanding and considerate of her husband's business. He recovered his potency. As Ogden Nash said: "Being a little incompatible is the spice of life, particularly if he has income and she is pattable."

Cures for Frigidity and Impotency

A woman's frigidity may stem from several causes: *organic* (injuries or illnesses in any part of the body; low androgen levels; vaginal lesions); *relational* (lack of love or intimacy between partners); or *psychological* (shame or guilt feelings; ignorance). Dr. Albert Ellis suggests that a woman can help herself overcome frigidity by following these suggestions:

1. Time sexual relations when both you and your partner desire it and have plenty of time and no distractions.

2. Experiment and determine what pleases you, and make sure these special erogenous zones have been properly stimulated. Even have the partner use lotions or ointments to properly massage these areas.

3. A *couple* of drinks may help, but don't overdo it.

4. Practice thinking of things that excite you—stories, pictures, past sex experiences—and keep your mind focused on these arousing subjects and events.

Even if a wife isn't the cause of her husband's impotency (or a husband of his wife's frigidity), there is much that one partner can do to help the other.

Perhaps the first step for a frigid or impotent person should be to have a complete physical. If the doctor diagnoses a hormonal or glandular deficiency, he could treat the physical cause.

But assuming that 95 percent or more of frigidity and impotency is emotionally caused, the couple must approach the problem both mentally and physically.

Assuming that a woman can be aroused, Dr. Ellis suggests the following steps for her and her mate to help her reach full climax:

1. The partner should exert steady, consistent, rhythmic pressure of those special areas of sex sensation, such as the clitoris and upper wall of the vagina. In some cases, special strokes—intermittent, irregular, forceful—may be desirable.

2. Verbalize expressions of love and passion.

3. Assume the most comfortable and stimulating position (usually with the woman on top).

4. Try various positions and multiple physical contact—such as the male's kissing or caressing his wife's breasts while having intercourse. (There's no law against a woman stimulating herself at the same time).

5. *Don't* try for simultaneous orgasms, especially if the woman has trouble reaching climax (more of this later).

In the man, erection takes place when his erection-control center sends enough signals (from mental and physical stimuli) to allow more blood to flow into the penis than flow out; the penis thus becomes larger and more rigid.

But if the psychological or reflex stimuli aren't maintained long enough—or if there is emotional or tactile interference—a man may lose his erection. When ejaculation takes place, erection subsides promptly because the sympathetic nerve impulses facilitate the emission of semen and simultaneously constrict the vessels supplying blood to the erectile tissues of the penis. Thus, both erection and ejaculation depend upon the right mental and physical stimuli.

Physically, a woman can help a man insert his penis if she bends her knees or elevates her pelvis by using a pillow.

A man can help himself to maintain an erection if he pulls his penis downward while partially erect (if the penis is pulled upward to the abdomen, it tends to relax). The man can also apply pressure or stimulation at the base of the penis to stimulate the major nerves and to hold in the proper amount of blood to maintain erection.

One experimental, and therefore rare, method of counteracting chronic impotence is the implantation of a "pacemaker" in the penis.

This pacemaker consists of two inflatable elongated silicone rubber cylinders with fluid stored in a reservoir implanted in the patient's pelvic area. The man controls the flow by squeezing one bulb, which pushes fluid into the cylinders and causes erection. To make the penis soft, the man merely squeezes the other bulb, sending fluid back into the reservoir. The device was developed and perfected by the urology service of St. Luke's Hospital (Houston, Texas), the division of urology of Baylor College of Medicine, and the departments of neurology, biomedical engineering, and mechanical engineering at the University of Minnesota. It has been implanted successfully in about ten men, one of whom is sixty-six years old.

Penis transplants may be possible in the future; experiments are now going on.

Dr. Bernard C. Gindes, a Beverly Hills, California phychiatrist, and Dr. Charles P. Ledergerber, assistant clinical professor of obstetrics and gynecology at the University of California Medical Center (Los Angeles), say they cure both frigidity and impotence through electro-acupuncture.

To cure impotence, the doctors insert seven needles (wired to a machine that gives a 9-volt charge) in the back, neck, and ear. For frigidity, they insert six needles at certain points in the abdomen and above the ankle. They give six to eight treatments over a three-week period, and they claim cures in about 83 percent of patients.

"With older persons," says Dr. Ledergerber, "it's often just the everyday strain." The treatments help to relax anxious and depressed patients.

The doctors believe that their treatment works by electrically stimulating the autonomic nervous system, which regulates the body's involuntary responses. Stimulating a peripheral point of the nervous system apparently causes a specific reflex that relaxes a certain organ or part of the body. The doctors also think the electro-acupuncture speeds up the body's production of electricity.

Whether it's the psychological boost of feeling helped or the boost of electricity, acupuncture may offer new hope for treating an old problem.

Doctors are also testing an artificial hormone, called LRF, that has been successful in inducing rats to mate. Two hours after injection, the rats (whose ovaries had been removed) became sexually stimulated, and the effect lasted for eight hours. This hormone is being tested for its effectiveness in impotent males.

A clever mistress once said: "You'd be surprised at how much a man can do with his hands." Humans are equipped with hands that can be gentle and caressing ... fingers that can be probing and stimulating. If a man learns to lovingly fondle a woman's breast ... manipulate her nipples with his fingers ... use his hands and fingers to stimulate the vulva and clitoral area ... he can make up for a weak or flaccid penis.

Masters and Johnson have proven that the female orgasm resulting from manual manipulation of breasts and clitoris is as good as—if not better than—orgasm resulting from actual vaginal intercourse.

Dr. Edwin W. Hirsch, author of *The Power of Love*, writes: "If a woman understands the role of the clitoris and the gratification that can emanate from deft manipulation of this all-important genital organ, as well as the feeling of her mate's closeness and ardor, she can by her participation dispel the feeling of sexual incompetence in her mate."

Some older men may have lost the ability to achieve a cerebral erection (mental stimulation) but they can still get a tactile or reflex erection through penis manipulation. A cooperative female can help her man achieve this erection if she knows how to handle and fondle the penis.

Marriage counselor Dr. Aaron L. Rutledge suggests that very often the problem with an older man is that he requires a *great deal* of stimulation or *very difficult* stimulation to become fully aroused. This can take the form of a woman's playing with or expressing curiosity about various parts of a man's body as well as exploring the various parts with hands, fingers, tongue.

By telling each other what pleases and stimulates, a man and a woman help each other to climax. This approach to lovemaking not only satisfies the wife but also provides the greatest possible stimulation to the husband. By witnessing mounting excitement in one partner, the other is swept along to climax.

This touching, feeling, and fondling goes beyond just the tactile sensations; it often opens the door to more psychological intimacy whereby a person not only learns what physically pleases the other person, but what pleases him/herself. It also eliminates the strain of performance and the inhibition of competition.

The Dual Problems of Premature Ejaculation

Premature ejaculation is probably the most common male sexual problem and one of the greatest causes of a woman's sexual unhappiness.

A man ejaculates prematurely in two ways: (1) *before* he introduces his penis into the vulva; (2) *shortly after* introducing the penis into the vulva and before the female has an orgasm.

Why does a man ejaculate prematurely? Prominent sexologists offer these explanations:

• *Hurried sexual relations.* Most premature ejaculators have had a history of earlier hurried sexual relations—hasty lovemaking in the back seat of a car, "fast tricks" with prostitutes. Perhaps the man even came to pride himself on his rabbitlike accomplishments.

A man's educational level may have something to do with premature ejaculation. As Masters and Johnson write in *Human Sexual Inadequacy*: "High school dropouts rarely complain about premature ejaculation—although their wives may."

• *Differences in timing.* Both men and women can reach orgasm within two to five minutes by masturbating. If the man is used to ejaculating through masturbation, he may not take the time to indulge the ten to fiteen minutes of foreplay (longer if there is not much clitoral stimulation) that the female needs to reach orgasm.

Kinsey believed that the time difference betweeen a woman's reaching orgasm by masturbation and by copulating comes about because she is less aroused than the male by visual stimuli, and more distracted by outside events and noises during intercourse.

• *Distractions during intercourse.* A ringing telephone or an awakened child quickly subdues passion. A woman needs continuous clitoral and other stimulation to lead to orgasm. If either partner is distracted and stops applying stimulation for even a few seconds, the woman loses her sensations of arousal. It's hard to "tune out" or ignore a ringing telephone or awakened child. About the only foolproof methods are to take the phone off the hook, lock the bedroom doors, or take a "second honeymoon" without the children.

• *Physical disorders.* Neglected gonorrhea, nonspecific urethritis and inflamed prostate (see above) can all cause premature ejaculation.

• *Hypersensitive nerves.* Some men may have a tight, unretractable, or oversensitive foreskin. If so, circumcision (at any age!) usually desensitizes the penis. By using a local anaesthetic on the penis head (see page 112) a man can make it less sensitive.

Treatments for Premature Ejaculation

Both partners suffer in premature ejaculation, and they may even blame each other for the condition. The wife may think the husband is selfish and inconsiderate; the man may feel the woman isn't patient or skillful enough to prevent this sexual mishap.

Actually, both may be right. The man may be selfish, but he may be so because of an upbringing that played down the need of satisfying a woman—or the fact that a woman even *wanted* to be satisfied. Women are just learning—and insisting—on their sexual "rights." Interestingly enough, this has increased the incidence of "youthful incompetence"—overeager or demanding females are *scaring* young partners into impotency or premature ejaculation. Between the old and new concepts lies a dearth of communication that aggravates this problem.

Most sexual therapists (especially Masters and Johnson) claim they can cure premature ejaculation (frigidity and impotency) by a combination of the following physical and psychological techniques:

1. *Learning to communicate.* The partners are first asked to concentrate on pleasing each other by touching (without intercourse) the genital areas and breasts. Once they have learned to communicate by touch, they are encouraged to verbalize these feelings. Father Andrew Greeley says that a man will not become a skillful lover until " . . . it becomes obvious to him that his wife hungers for his body, because in perceiving that hunger he perceives, perhaps for the first time, his worth as a sexual creature."

2. *Ejaculatory training control.* The woman is instructed to sit on the bed, leaning comfortably on a pillow and supported by the headboard. The man, lying on his back, facing her, positions his body between her legs, with his feet placed outside her thighs. Then, by caressing the penis, the woman encourages erection. As soon as the man gets an erection, the woman "moderates" it by using the "squeeze technique." She holds the penis between the thumb and the first two fingers of the same hand. Her thumb is placed on the underside of the penis, where the shaft ends and the penis head begins. Her two fingers are placed on the opposite side from the thumb, one on each side of the ridge separating the glans from the shaft. The woman then squeezes fairly hard for three or four seconds. The pressure makes the man lose his urge to ejaculate and may also cause him to lose his erection. After fifteen to twenty seconds, the woman repeats the procedure, until it becomes easy to have fifteen to twenty minutes of continuous sex play without

ejaculation.

3. *Special positions.* The woman sits on top ("female superior position"), which reduces the man's urge to ejaculate and gives the woman pelvic (thrusting) control. After she has applied the squeeze technique, the woman inserts the penis into the vagina. But instead of doing it hastily, she glides it in, parting her vaginal lips with her thumbs, lightly taking the penis between her two forefingers, and guiding it to the vagina entrance.

The woman then makes nondemanding pelvic thrusts, rotating or swinging her hips sideways, but not up and down. She can also apply the squeeze techniques if the man signals that he is about to ejaculate.

Once the couple has mastered this technique, the man is permitted to thrust lightly to maintain erection. But the couple should be able to stay in the female superior position for fifteen to twenty minutes without ejaculation.

After control increases, the couple is encouraged to move into the lateral (side-by-side) position, in which the female can still control the pelvic thrusting (especially if the man holds his pubic bone firmly against the partner's clitoral area). The man can rotate his pelvis or swing his hips from side to side; this quickly stimulates the woman, particularly if she rotates her pelvis or swings her hips in the opposite direction.

4. *Desensitizing the penis.* If a man's penis is wet, it is less sensitive. Therefore, a man can lubricate his penis with an anesthetic ointment or an aeresol spray anesthetic. Dr. Robert Chartham, author of *The Sensuous Couple*, recommends that a man use an anesthetic spray twenty minutes before lovemaking (it takes this long for the spray to take effect). The anesthetic effect lasts about forty minutes; it doesn't interfere with erection, orgasm, or ejaculation.

5. *Using tranquilizers.* Some doctors suggest the use of tranquilizers to prevent premature ejaculation. Dr. Chartham has made tests using the drug Valium, and has found that five milligrams taken thirty minutes before lovemaking calms the man, relieves his anxiety, and allows him to control orgasm and ejaculation.

Other doctors recommend tranquilizers containing chlor-promazine, chlordiazepoxide (Librium), and phenelzine (Nardil). A tranquilizing sex pill has been tested in England. It consists of a drug, cyproterone acetate, that apparently suppresses the activity of the hypothalamus, which serves as a message conductor from the brain to the sex glands. The drug blocks the number of messages going through, thereby reducing the amount of male hormones secreted into the bloodstream.

6. *Mental exercises.* Some men say they try doing complicated mathematical problems mentally, or silently reciting the alphabet backwards. But these methods may not be completely successful, or may work only temporarily. Other men say they can hold back on ejaculation by tensing the buttocks muscles and tightening the muscles of the anus and rectum.

7. *Prostate treatment.* Prostate disorders often cause—and result from—premature ejaculation. One doctor told of a sixty-eight-year-old widower who had been sexually abstinent for the five years following his wife's death, resuming sexual activity only when he met a forty-two-year-old divorcée. Their initial sexual relations were successful; however, after about a month the man began to ejaculate prematurely. A few weeks later he noticed blood in his ejaculate; a medical examination detected an enlarged prostate.

Doctors treat premature ejaculation linked to prostate trouble as a prostate problem. They cure the prostatic disease with anitbiotics or other therapy, and the premature ejaculation usually vanishes. If the prostatic disorder is the result of premature ejaculation (rather than the cause), the doctors try to uncover any situational or emotional problems the man may have.

Sometimes premature ejaculation is a sign of general ill health, and improving the general health will help the situation. Sometimes premature ejaculation stems from deep-seated fear or hatred of women, and the man may need psychiatric treatment.

But every man suffers from premature ejaculation at some time, especially if he is worried or fatigued. If it happens only occasionally, there's no real problem.

Causes and Cures of Ejaculatory Incompetence

Ejaculatory incompetence—the inability to ejaculate in the vagina—is the opposite of premature ejaculation. The man with ejaculatory incompetence is able to have and maintain an erection and keep his penis inside the vagina for thirty minutes to an hour, but he has a mental block against allowing his seminal fluid to enter the vagina.

Strangely, most of these men can masturbate or be manipulated (manually or orally) to ejaculation.

Many factors contribute to this condition, including religious restrictions, fear of impregnating, lack of physical interest, or active dislike for the female partner. Such dislike might be the problem when the partner is a dominant female or one whom the man sees as a threat either to his virility or to his traditional male role. Masters and Johnson tell of one man who married for money and social position, but who just couldn't get excited enough (or felt threatened enough) by his wife to ejaculate intravaginally with her. This man, like others, could ejaculate with a partner he "liked" or one he didn't feel as a threat.

Physical causes of ejaculatory incompetence can include general fatigue, illness, too frequent stimulation, and ejaculation in too short a time. Rest or convalescence will usually soon restore virility.

In psychologically caused ejaculatory incompetence, the man may require psychotherapy. Masters and Johnson have cured ejaculatory incompetence by instructing the woman to ejaculate the man in ways he finds most exciting (manually or orally). The idea is for him to identify ejaculation with the pleasure the woman gives him, so that he no longer regards her as a threat.

After she has learned to masturbate the man, the woman continues stimulating the penis, then places it in the vagina just before ejaculation. She assumes the female superior position, kneeling over the man who is lying on his back, with her knees outside his thighs. Once she has inserted the penis, she moves demandingly until he ejaculates. After the first ejaculatory success, the man and woman learn how to prolong the time the penis is in the vagina, so that the woman can reach orgasm before the man ejaculates.

The important factor is communication—in feeling as well as in verbalizing. If couples can be encouraged to express feelings of love and consideration, they create a favorable climate for correcting any sexual problems.

Ejaculation Without Orgasm

The *British Medical Journal* of March 31, 1973, carried a doctor's question about recommended treatment for a fit man of fifty who was capable of normal sexual activity but didn't have an orgasm when he ejaculated.

The *Journal's* authorities suggested that the doctor take a complete case history to see if there were any personal or relational problems that could account for increasing anxiety, changes in mood (depression), or excessive preoccupation with aging. They suggested that the man's wife be questioned separately to get her views on any problems or changes.

The *Journal* went on: "Though antidepressant therapy and/or medication may be helpful, the basic treatment is psychotherapeutic—either individual, group, marital, or behavioral. The outlook for this type of problem is good if it is tackled energetically."

Surrogate Sex, Anyone?

At one time, Masters and Johnson used volunteer sexual surrogates (substitute sexual partners) to help in their therapy (mainly with men). Most of the surrogates were office girls or nurses who had experienced "sexually oriented trauma" and had humanistic yearnings to create a healthier sexual world. Masters and Johnson stopped using surrogates, apparently because of a lawsuit brought against them by the husband of a woman suspected of being a surrogate.

In many cities, however, individual and clinical surrogate partners are available.

Who are these surrogates? Among women, are they prostitutes who exchange sexual services for money? *New York* magazine recently interviewed a female surrogate; basically, here is her story.

She's in her thirties, divorced, and a mother. She became sexually emancipated in college where she ran a sex-information clinic. Now she takes referrals from various physicians and psychiatrists around Manhattan. The surrogate started charging $500 for twelve sessions, but she has since raised her fee to $750 with no decrease in business. She points out that she charges less than call girls.

Her first session is a "social occasion," in which she meets the man for dinner and dancing so they can get to know each other. Then she holds a "sensate focus" session, in which they stroke each other nonsexually. Only then does she proceed to step-by-step sexual activity to cure the premature ejaculation or impotency. During intercourse she strives to make the man feel easy inside her vagina; later she progresses to thrusting in the female superior position.

She says: "Nothing could be less romantic, even less sexual, than being a surrogate. It's very manipulative ... it's as if you were giving lessons in tennis."

However, this woman looks upon herself as a crusader for sexual freedom. Although she receives referrals from physicians and therapists, she doesn't work in conjunction with other professionals.

There *are* call girls who act as surrogates. In her book

Psycho-Sexual Transition, Martha Stein, a young social worker, advocates call-girl surrogates because she has found that many prostitutes are supportive and therapeutic when confronted with timid or impotent males. But many call girls don't like the supervision and "paper work" that would be entailed if they worked for a clinic.

Miss Stein found that the call girls helped their clients by emotional satisfaction as well as sexual fulfillment. She said: "The call girls, by providing the clients with satisfaction important to their sense of well-being, functioned effectively as professional therapists."

Masters and Johnson said they didn't want to use call girls as surrogates because " . . . to have used prostitutes would have been at best clinically unsuccessful and at worst psychologically disastrous."

Sexual surrogates' may be more numerous than you think. In California male and female surrogates banded together to form the first national surrogate's association. There are enough of them to lobby in the state legislature to get licenses. Most of these surrogates view themselves as dedicated and serving mankind.

Who are the clients? Mostly professional businessmen and well educated. Norman C. King, who is building a chain of Male Potency Centers of America, said he made a mailing to 1,500 Wall Street executives earning over $40,000 asking if they would be interested in sexual-surrogate services (supposedly for any problem they might have). He claims that one-fourth of the men actually telephoned to ask about his services.

In this chapter we have examined some emotional causes of frigidity, impotency, premature ejaculation, and ejaculatory incompetence. In the next chapter we shall examine some medical and physical reasons for these problems—especially what happens sexually if you have an illness or an operation. We shall also explore ways in which you can help yourself overcome any handicaps and problems.

IX
ILLNESS, SURGERY, AND
WHAT OTHER PROBLEMS?

No illness results from merely growing older. But the more years we live, the more exposed we are to our polluted environment, the ravages of certain chemicals or drugs, stresses and diseases that bombard our system, and surgery—all of which could affect our sexual lives.

As we discussed in the last chapter, many doctors feel that sexual abstinence causes problems. That's why most doctors urge that couples resume normal sexual relations as soon as possible after illness or surgery.

Dr. John F. Oliven, author of *Sexual Hygiene and Pathology*, suggests the greatest possible sexual freedom at the earliest possible time compatible with the illness and treatment.

Resuming sexual activities as soon as possible minimizes strains on the marriage and furthers the health and well-being of each partner. In fact, sexual activity in many cases is a therapy and a preventive of many common health problems in later years.

What are some common illnesses that could affect sexual activity? Among them are heart disease (including angina), arthritis, diabetes, epilepsy, Peyronie's disease, gout, emphysema, nerve problems, stroke, and venereal diseases.

What are some of the common physical and surgical problems that could affect sexual activity? Among them are backache; headache; prostate, rectal, and colonic surgery; hysterectomy and other vaginal surgery; breast surgery; and various physical conditions that could cause pain in intercourse.

Allergies and exposure to pesticides, radiation, and pollution all affect our sex lives. Then, of course, we're affected by certain common drugs such as sleeping tablets, tranquilizers, caffeine, tobacco, alcohol, and perhaps the more esoteric narcotics (sometimes contained in medicines)—morphine, opium, or cocaine.

The longer we live, the more likely we are to be exposed to

these negative influences and the less likely we are to withstand them—as we did when younger. Surgery can be especially dangerous to sexual performance, because many patients conclude (incorrectly) that the operation in some way has altered their body functions and impaired their sexual performance.

In a survey by physicians at Temple University School of Medicine, 78 percent of patients (medical or surgical) reported a decline in the frequency of sexual activity following disability. Other patients said that they changed their sexual patterns and that they experienced less satisfaction and interest. Thirty-six percent indicated a desire for more satisfaction in their present sexual activity, and 42 percent believed their spouses presently desired more sexual satisfaction.

In some cases the patient must take special measures—lubricants, new positions, restraint, or modification—to reach orgasm and ejaculation. In most cases your doctor should be able to advise and prescribe some technique or medicine that might help. And drugstores sell vaginal creams and lubricants that make intercourse easier.

In the following sections we shall discuss some common problems and what you can do to overcome them to renew sexual relations as soon as possible.

"My Aching Back" Is a Poor Excuse

Some persons may use a backache to avoid sex. One doctor told of a successful fifty-six-year-old businessman whose backache didn't respond to normal treatment. In further questioning, the doctor found that the man used his back pain (which was real enough) to avoid intercourse. When the patient found the courage to face up to his marital and emotional conflicts, his back pain disappeared.

Whether back pain is physically or emotionally induced, the pain inhibits or prevents sexual movements. In the basic intercourse movement—the pelvic thrust—the participant uses his lower abdominal and buttock muscles. If this thrust strains a damaged back, it can cause muscle spasms and pain. Conversely, the sexual pelvic thrust strengthens back muscles and is an excellent backache preventive.

Dr. Lawrence W. Friedmann, medical director of the Institute for Crippled and Disabled, Research Rehabilitation Center, New York City, points out that sexual activity won't adversely affect a person with back pain. He says: "A person with back pain need not fear that sex, somehow, may inflict some permanent damage. The problem lies in finding some way to satisfy, physically and emotionally, both the patient with pain and the partner. Any way may be used if it satisfies both partners and is not offensive to either."

Dr. Friedmann has these suggestions for satisfactory sexual relations during back problems:

• Before sex, the patient could take a hot bath or apply heat to reduce discomfort. He/she could also take an analgesic (aspirin in some form) about forty-five minutes before the sex act (to give it time to work). Gentle massage could also help ease discomfort and could be a good prelude to making love.

• During sex, the injured partner should lie on his back. The other partner should be on top and control the thrusting. In some cases, this could work if the couple lie side-by-side and the "well" partner does the thrusting.

• If any movement causes the patient pain, the couple might use mutual masturbation, accompanied by warmth and tenderness.

• If the patient suffers a muscle spasm after sexual activity, heat, brief massage, and aspirin might help. But the relaxation that follows sexual activity may ease any muscle spasm that had been bothersome prior to sex.

Dr. Friedmann ends on a cheerful note: "Actually, sexual activity at times when acute back pain isn't present can be looked upon validly as an aid in overcoming the cause of the back problem and minimizing future attacks of acute pain."

"The World's Greatest Excuse"

"Not tonight, I have a headache," has been called "the world's greatest excuse." Your brain is your main sex organ, and it has its ups and downs—like other sex organs.

Doctors divide "sexual headaches" into two categories: *before* and *after.* The "before" headache is often an excuse to avoid sex—like the backache. The pain may be real but the reason may be obscure: conflicts between fear and desire; desire for affection rather than physical activity.

The "after" headache stems from more complex causes. In a typical case, a woman gets a headache within a minute or two after having an orgasm. One patient said: It's a severe hard throbbing which hurts all over—it hits over **and** behind the right eye, and it can last an hour or more. If I go to sleep it clears up and is gone when I awake." There is usually no nausea or vomiting with this type of headache.

A person who has reached a peak of sexual excitement but failed to have an orgasm might have a similar headache.

Doctors have several theories for the "after" headaches. Cornell psychiatrist Dr. Dorothea Kerr believes that the headache is emotionally based because, "People have a lot of guilt feelings after intercourse." Dr. Harry H. Gerner, head of the neurology and psychiatry department of the Chicago Medical School, thinks that the brain becomes engorged and distended with blood; this in-and-out pouring of blood could produce symptoms seen in migraine and other vascular headaches.

If you or your partner experience headaches before or after intercourse, Dr. Bernard J. Baltes, codirector of the Mt. Sinai Headache Clinic (Chicago), suggests taking ergotamine (a favorite drug for migraine) as a preventive before sexual activity. Dr. Maurice J. Martin, a Mayo Clinic psychiatrist, found that some three-quarters of his patients suffering from tension headaches had sexual conflicts—premature ejaculation, pain in intercourse, impotency, frigidity, or aversion to sex. Perhaps some of these problems can be solved physically, but most of them are psychological or emotional.

Fat People Miss More than Good Looks
If you're too fat, not only does your sex life suffer, but you are a prime candidate for arthritis, diabetes, and other illnesses. Fat can also disturb endocrine glands and decrease secretions of testes and suprarenal glands, causing diminished sex drive.

In the Middle Ages ladies dined separately from men because it was believed the movement of their jaws in chewing detracted from their sex appeal.

Maybe so, but a study conducted at the State University of New York Upstate Medical Center found that sexual responsiveness in female subjects was "positively and significantly correlated" with their positive attitude toward food and eating. And a British psychiatrist found that the divorce rate is as much as 84 percent higher in countries where wives count calories—probably because frustration with diets interfered with sexual enjoyment. Also, experiments at the University of Minnesota proved that a semistarvation diet may make you sexually indifferent.

Regardless of these plusses for food (not necessarily for fat), excessive weight inhibits good sexual relations because it's inefficient, unappealing, and makes it harder for couples to "get together."

A trim, fit body helps sex. The same study that found the correlation between eating and sex also found that women who don't exercise are less sexually responsive than those who like physical activity.

When Should the Heart Rule the Head?

Dr. Jeremiah Stamler, director of the Chicago Coronary Prevention Evaluation Program, points out that 50 percent of heart attacks occur during rest or sleep—only 2 percent occur during strenuous activity. Taking that a step further: only about 1 percent of sudden coronary deaths occur during intercourse.

Doctors add that the physical stress of sexual relations is approximately equal to a brisk walk down the street. According to Dr. Philip Reichert, former executive secretary, American College of Cardiology, "We must rid ourselves of the notion that every heart patient lives under an overhanging sword and that he faces the constant threat of sudden death. The congenial married couple, accustomed to each other and whose technique is habituated through many years of companionship, can achieve sexual satisfaction without too great an expenditure of body energy or too severe a strain upon the heart ... "

But he warns: "The situation is quite different in the case of a prowling bachelor picking up a stranger and taking her furtively to a hotel. Here are the excitement of the chase, the lure of the unknown, the pressure and preening of courtship compressed into a fleeting hour, which may have tragic consequences for the sufferer from heart disease."

Another prominent heart specialist, Dr. Edward Weiss, points out that emotional tension arising out of sexual tension may precede a coronary attack or it may complicate the patient's recovery.

More and more physicians are realizing that hypertension resulting from sexual frustration may be more damaging than the emotional tension induced by sexual intercourse itself.

But although physicians may give a coronary patient standard advice on smoking, drinking, eating, many fail to give advice or information on sexual activity. Dr. Elliott M. Feigenbaum, Medical Director, Western Institute of Human Resources, points out that most coronary patients are over age fifty, but two-thirds have received no advice regarding sexual activity from their physician, and the other third report that the advice was vague or nonspecific.

In a typical example, one doctor told a coronary patient that he could resume sexual activity "when he felt up to it." Two years later he saw the patient, who looked miserable. Asked what was wrong, the man said he hadn't had sexual relations in two years because he "didn't know if he felt up to it."

Now most doctors specify that most patients can safely resume sexual activity six to eight weeks after an acute coronary occlusion if there has been no subsequent anginal pain. For patients with persisting symptoms, drugs and physical-fitness programs can improve sexual and working performance. Eventually, 80 to 90 percent of heart attack patients should be able to enjoy a full sex life.

Most doctors caution patients to perform sexual intercourse initially in positions not requiring arm support; e.g., side-by-side or female on top. These positions also require much less body thrusting by the male (assuming he's the heart patient). Additional precautions may include that sex take place in the morning rather than at night and that intercourse not take place with a full stomach, when wearing constrictive garments, or under unusual conditions of heat, cold, or humidity. Doctors also caution against abrupt withdrawal (coitus interruptus) or any other sudden strain.

One reason that more doctors are "prescribing" sexual relations is that laboratory studies have shown that it's not the physical strain of sexual intercourse that causes problems, but rather the emotional surges that bring about a rise in heart rate and blood pressure. Even so, heart rates monitored during sexual intercourse show that the heart rate responses are similar to those observed in the same individuals during regular daily activity such as driving a car, discussing business, or climbing one or two flights of stairs.

Dr. Robert A. Miller, director of the Coronary Care Unit at the Naples (Florida) Medical Center, says that many persons are afraid to have sexual relations following a heart attack because they may develop strange symptoms: minor chest discomfort, rapid pulse, slight shortness of breath. If they have had angina pains following the attack, intercourse may bring on the pains.

However, the doctor feels that the heart patient can avoid angina pains by taking a nitroglycerine pill before intercourse, and that by physical training most people can gradually reduce the rapid pulse that occurs with exercise.

Dr. Miller adds: " ... undertaking each new activity during heart convalescence is an experiment to see how the heart is going to react. Just as you report to your physician the effect that walking up the first flight of stairs has on your heart, you should tell him if you feel strange in any way during intercourse. There is a good chance that there may be a simple remedy for your problem; the remedy may simply consist of reassurance."

Other doctors feel that discomfort should be the deciding factor as to whether sexual activity is permissible for heart patients.

Doctor Miller (like other doctors) warns heart patients against drinking too much before sex. Although a drink or two may relax the patient, too much alcohol may make it more difficult to reach ejaculation or orgasm and may turn an enjoyable experience into an exhausting marathon.

Dr. Albert Ellis, writing in *Sex and the Heart*, says: "Stop believing, on the one hand, that a person must have intercourse to prove his (masculinity) or her (femininity); and, on the other hand, that it is wrong or harmful to have sex urges . . . try to satisfy your partner sexually, but don't literally kill yourself trying."

What about sex after a stroke? Dr. John E. Sarno, director of Outpatient Services at the Institute of Rehabilitation Medicine, New York, reports that an occasional stroke patient will have increased desire for sex, and he says: "It demonstrates that having a stroke is not necessarily associated with changes for the worse in a person's sexual life." He also adds that there is no evidence that sexual activity may retard recovery from a stroke, but be cautious that any problems or doubts should be discussed with the doctor.

Is Arthritis A Problem?

Although arthritis isn't aggravated by the sex act, it may cause sexual problems. One doctor tells of a patient who came to see him because he felt he was no longer a man but a hopeless, helpless cripple, a burden to his wife because of his arthritis.

The doctor told the man to try intercourse while lying on his side (the man suffered from back pains and spinal problems). At first the patient was reluctant to try this, but then he found the position was satisfactory to him and acceptable to his wife, as was the female-on-top position. As the patient improved and his back straightened, he felt free to try previously preferred positions. But now he knows that whenever his back bothers him he need not curtail his marital relations.

In counseling arthritis patients, doctors stress these points:

• Patients with arthritis must learn to handle sex functions just as they do homemaking, holding a job, shopping, and practically all other daily activities.

• Ideally, sexual activity should be planned in advance for the hours when the patient feels most rested.

• Times to be avoided are periods of fatigue that follow high energy outputs.

• Medication, hot showers, alcohol, pleasant music, and any other techniques generally utilized to reduce tension can enhance pleasure. Any measure that reduces pain, fear of pain, or fear of causing pain will promote relaxation in both partners.

• Women are advised to identify the coital positions in which they feel most comfortable.

There is some evidence that sexual activity helps arthritis, probably because of adrenal-gland production of cortisone. The sexual act is itself a form of physical activity, helping people stay in good physical health, and to reduce tensions, which are both physical and psychological.

A Sexual Diet for Diabetes?

Diabetes is a failure in body chemistry in which the body cannot handle some foods we eat—mainly starches and sugars. Although the cause of diabetes is unknown, emotional factors— including sex—can contribute to it.

Doctors estimate that half of all diabetic men complain of impotence, and this might be the first symptom that brings the diabetic to medical attention. Dr. Flanders Dunbar, a specialist in diabetes, adds that many diabetics were "spoiled children," and that their marriages aren't outstandingly successful because the diabetic partner often wants to be babied more than usual.

Besides impotency, other symptoms of diabetes include increased thirst, constant hunger, frequent urination, weight loss, itching, easy tiring, changes in vision, and slow healing of cuts. Diabetes can also cause retrograde ejaculation, as described in the section on prostate surgery.

Just why does diabetes cause impotency and other sexual problems? Some doctors suggest that the disease hardens the muscles of the reproductive tract and the walls of the seminal vesicles and sperm ducts. Most doctors say it may cause degeneration of the nerve fibers responsible for erection.

It doesn't follow, however, that the average man who contracts diabetes becomes impotent or that the illness was aggravated by a sexual disorder. Other factors than bodily changes may play a significant role in bringing about impotency in diabetes.

With treatment and control consisting of planned diet, exercise, and insulin shots or oral medication, most diabetics can lead useful and active lives—including sexual.

Progress with Peyronie's Disease

Some older men may suffer from a little-known but increasingly common ailment called Peyronie's disease. In this problem, the penis is bowed upward and angled to the right or left. The curvature is produced by a saddle-shaped fibrous body on the upper side of the penis, which does not expand when erection occurs. This can cause difficult or painful intercourse, although only occasionally does it cause impotency.

The condition may be caused by trauma, possibly sexually oriented. Many patients have first noticed this disease after the death or serious illness of the wife, or after some other condition that caused abstinence.

Doctors have tried, with limited success, X-ray and radium therapy, electrolysis, Vitamin E, cortisone and even surgery. However, the problem usually limits itself and may even disappear in about four years.

How Various Types of Surgery Affect Sexual Functioning

When she was clinical professor of obstetrics and gynecology at the New York University School of Medicine, the late Dr. Sophia J. Kleegman told this story:

"I was doing a vaginal plastic operation when my chief cautioned me: 'Watch out. Not only does your patient need good pelvic support, but she also needs room enough left for sex life.'

"But this patient is fifty-six years old!" I said, thinking to myself: 'Sex at her age?' My chief, who was also fifty-six, reminded me that sex does not end in the fifties. This knowledge was of great benefit to all my future older patients."

It's true that not too many years ago, when an older person had to have surgery in and around the genital and pelvic areas, doctors paid little or no attention to the possible effects of the operation on sexual functioning. But today, when operations after age sixty on the prostate and womb are quite common, medical journals are alerting physicians to take sexual functioning into consideration before, during, and after surgery.

In the previous chapter we discussed the effects of prostate surgery on sexual functioning. Here we shall mention only a study of sexual performance after prostatectomy made by surgeons at the University of California School of Medicine. Of 101 patients who had been operated on by one doctor during the previous five years, approximately 70 percent retained their sexual ability. "In general," concluded the surgeons, "there was surprisingly little post-prostatectomy impotency, regardless of the type of surgery, in men who were previously potent."

Surgery for prostate cancer sometimes requires removal of the testes and estrogen (female hormone) therapy. Drs. William J. Ellis and John T. Grayhack, reporting in the *Journal of Urology*, told of studies made of the sexual functioning of 82 patients, most of whom were between sixty and eighty-three. Of those who were potent before treatment (46 percent), approximately 50 percent maintained some degree of normal sexual activity. In fact, one sixty-two-year-old man whose testes were removed and who was also put on female hormone treatment had intercourse fifteen times a week after the treatment!

The story may be somewhat different for patients undergoing rectal surgery (for cancer) or for ulcerative colitis. One author found that potency was lost in 56 percent of 41 patients following removal of the rectum and retained in only 12 percent. On the other hand, among 95 patients who underwent rectal surgery for cancer, 72 percent retained erections, 64 percent could have intercourse, and 61 percent had undisturbed ejaculation. Among 21 other patients who underwent rectum removal because of ulcerative colitis, only two had sexual difficulty.

In cases where the person had a colostomy, or artificial anus, the patient feared the colostomy bag might slip during intercourse and cause messy smearing. Dr. Charles J. Weigel, addressing the International Academy of Proctology, said: "While colostomy restricts sexual relations, where the relationship was good prior to the onset of impotency, the emotional rapport continues to be good between husband and wife. In the case of pleasureless and unstable marriages before the advent of colostomy, the emotional relationship deteriorates and the colostomy is used as a rationalization for the situation."

How Does Hysterectomy Affect Sexual Functioning?

There is no evidence that hysterectomy—with or without removal of the ovaries—changes sexual desire or performance, unless the change is psychological. Some women may feel "castrated"—they can no longer function as women. They may fear becoming unattractive, aging prematurely, and developing masculine characteristics.

These feelings may be hard for men to understand. One man asked a woman who just had a hysterectomy, "What do you need the uterus for?" The woman replied bitterly, "What do you need that thing for?" (pointing to *his* genital area).

Drs. Ralph M. Patterson and James B. Craig, of the Columbus Psychiatric Institute of Ohio State University, studied the psychological effects of hysterectomy on 100 women and found that 62 percent hadn't noticed any change at all and 20 of the women reported an increased sexual drive. Of the 18 who reported decreased desire, the investigators found other factors: 5 had experienced severe domestic stress, 1 had an impotent husband, 1 husband had committed incest, and 6 of the women had been frigid before. Concluded the psychiatrists: "In no instance were we able to demonstrate that the hysterectomy had any causal relationship to a decrease of erotic drive."

Another point of reassurance for women: no physiologic or anatomical changes take place in hysterectomy that should impair sexual satisfaction. Actual photographs of what happens during intercourse have shown that it is the lower third of the vagina—which is not involved in the surgery—that plays a basic part in sexual response.

In fact, after a hysterectomy, a doctor may do preventive surgery as a precaution against general relaxing of the vaginal walls. One woman who had this type of surgery says she now feels that she "can compete with any twenty-five-year-old."

It is essential that a woman's husband and other close persons know what to expect after a hysterectomy. As one doctor says: "...if a significant person in the social group of the hysterectomized woman falsely defines the woman as 'desexed,' 'neuter,' 'shell of a woman,' 'promiscuous' (the operation is punishment for sexual sins), the rejected or devalued woman may eventually behave in such a way that the originally false evaluation comes true." Or what sociologists call "a self-fulfilling prophecy."

How Other Vaginal Surgery Affects Husbands and Wives

Other vaginal surgery may also affect a couple's sexual happiness. Probably the most common surgical treatment for middle aged and older women involves prolapse (falling down or slipping out of place) of the uterus (or womb). In some women, prolapse may be without symptoms; other women may complain of a dragging feeling in the lower abdomen or vagina, a feeling of a descending lump, constipation, incontinence, backache.

This falling down or slipping of the uterus isn't fatal, and it might be better to have the symptoms alleviated rather than "cured" through surgery. In some cases, surgery might interfere with future sexual relations. One doctor tells of an eighty-two-year-old woman whose uterus prolapsed into the vagina and was causing all kinds of problems. The doctor had to tell her that the only answer was extensive surgery, including removal of the vagina (eliminating future sex relations). Her decision surprised even her doctor: she flatly refused to have any surgery done. According to her, she had always had a good sex life and she wasn't about to give it up now. She would somehow learn to handle the incontinence and other problems, but she was going to keep her vagina—and her sex life!

Her decision may have been wise. Two British physicians, W.J.A. Francis and T.N.A. Jeffcoate, estimate that approximately 20 percent of women who have repair for prolapse will suffer loss of feeling or pain in intercourse because the vagina becomes too narrow or because of tender scars. The narrowing may result partly from wasting away (atrophy) of the tissues of the vagina and partly from the sewing up of the vagina. Some patients also avoid sexual relations after these operations because they are afraid they'll be hurt.

However, skillful surgery can avoid shortening the vagina, and six weeks after the operation the physician can reexamine the patient and give specific instructions about resumption of intercourse.

How Breast Surgery Affects Sexual Desire

Cancer of the breast is the most common cause of death in women from forty to forty-four, and the risk increases with age. Some 85 percent of women treated by surgery when the cancer is still confined to the breast are free of disease five years later; but only 53 percent remain disease-free that long if the cancer had spread to the lymph glands in the armpit.

That's why it's so important for women (and men, too) to consult a doctor when they notice a thickening or lump in the breast. Not all lumps are cancerous, but some may be.

Woman should learn breast self-examination. If you haven't learned the right methods, ask your doctor. Or you may be near one of the twenty breast-screening clinics sponsored by the American Cancer Society and the National Cancer Institute, offering free examinations to women thirty-five years of age and older. These clinics have sophisticated diagnostic equipment (X-ray, xeroradiography, or thermography) that can detect the smallest lesion, not palpable even to the skilled physician.

If you should require surgery (either simple removal of the breast or radical mastectomy which also includes removal of some chest and underarm muscles and lymph glands), ask your doctor to explain the procedures and possible complications, if any. Dr. George Crile, Jr., of Cleveland Clinic Hospital, claims a 70 percent cure rate by removing *only* the lump and not the breast. His method has stirred much controversy, but it is a *possibility* in mastectomy.

After breast surgery, some women feel they've lost their beauty and sexual desire and desirability. Drs. Martha Schon and Arthur M. Sutherland, as part of a public health project, reported on the sexual life of 23 women (average age fifty-one) who had surgical removal of their breasts. Out of 22 who had sexual desire before the operation, 19 retained the same degree of desire after surgery, 2 reported a slight decrease, and 1 was uncertain because she felt too embarrassed, with only one breast, to resume sexual activity. Three out of four women reported that, after the operation, they received the same intensity of pleasure and gratification as before.

Often, as part of breast surgery, doctors remove the ovaries and adrenal glands, which secrete female hormones, and the pituitary gland, which stimulates secretions by these other glands. Ovary removal doesn't alter sexual response, but adrenal or pituitary removal may decrease sex drive. These glands produce testosterone, the male sex hormone that is said to be responsible for the sex drive in both men and women.

However, doctors can artificially replace this hormone; in some cases in which the male sex hormone has been used in massive doses as part of the treatment, women have experienced increased libido.

Since her mastectomy several years ago, one woman reports two rather torrid love affairs and now is happily married to a high government official. From what she says, neither she nor the men in her life have been unduly disturbed by the fact that "something is missing." She is charming and "sexy" in other ways, so men can well overlook this "problem."

When sexual function decreased after adrenal removal, the doctors report this decrease was offset by increased affection if a good husband-wife relationship existed before the operation. When the marriage had been unsatisfactory before the operation, the relationship seemed to deteriorate even further after surgery.

Causes and Cures of Painful Intercourse

Women complain more about painful intercourse than men. In women, the pain may be caused by physical and/or emotional problems. In men, the cause is usually physical.

Here is a brief rundown of problems and some suggested treatments:

• *Aching, burning, itching during intercourse.* This may be caused by lack of lubrication, either through failure to be aroused or—most likely in the menopausal years—dryness or thickness of the vaginal walls (see Chapter V). If vaginal tightness or lack of lubrication cause problems, you can use estrogenic creams or suppositories to moisten mucuouslinings of the vagina.

• *Infection in the vagina.* The vagina's natural acidity protects it against infection. But too frequent douching (which removes the acid) or a hormonal imbalance (making the vagina less acid) can make the vagina more vulnerable to bacterial or fungal growth. Vaginal contamination usually comes from the rectum, hands, clothing, or a foreign substance. Bacterial infections are the most common, especially *trichomonal* and *monilial.*

If the bacterial infection comes from the rectum (perhaps caused by a penis or finger that have been there) the couple can prevent this by *not* inserting a finger or penis in the vagina after it has been in the rectum, or by washing the parts first.

A trichomonal infection produces a cream-colored or bloody discharge, pain, and burning. Symptoms usually show up in the woman, although they may have been passed by an affected male who had no symptoms. A doctor can dry out the tissues affected by blowing a powdered chemical into the vagina. Or he can prescribe tablets or suppositories. A preferred treatment is to have both partners take a drug called Flagyl orally three times a day for ten days. Not everyone can tolerate Flagyl (it can cause nausea or diarrhea), but a doctor can also apply vaginal therapy by using white vinegar, boric acid, or lactic acid to suppress the trichomonas germs. If a man can't take the drug, the standard procedure is to do nothing; after a while the parasites will pass out of the body. Until a laboratory report confirms this, however, the man should avoid sexual intercourse.

Doctors also treat monilial infection with similar drugs and treatments. This infection causes swelling and weeping of the soft tissues as well as intense burning and itching, which may make for painful intercourse and urination.

Woman may also have pain in the outer vagina, the clitoris, or deep in the cervix. Such pain may stem from local irritations, chemicals (contraceptives), or physical obstructions or complications following an operation, or because of tumors, cysts, or venereal disease. Needless to say, any woman who has a vaginal discharge, pain, or sore on or near her genital area should have an examination. Once detected, these problems can be cured by medical treatment.

In men, painful intercourse can be caused by:

• *Hypersensitive glans.* In some men the penis head becomes extremely tender after ejaculation, and they must withdraw it from the vagina. Sometimes allergic reactions to contraceptive creams, jellies, foams, and douches causes the sensitivity. The solution then is to change the contraceptive method or preparation. If the man is not circumcised, he can get occasional relief by pulling the foreskin well back over the penis head.

• *Poor hygiene.* In men who aren't circumcised, debris may collect under the foreskin and become infected, causing inflammation and irritation. The best preventive is to pull the foreskin back and wash the penis head and underskin with soap and water. A better solution: Circumcision (at any age).

• *Infections.* A man may become infected with gonorrhea from a woman who has no symptoms. The first symptoms in a man occur three to nine days after infection and include itching or burning upon urination and a puslike discharge from the urinary canal. Any man with these symptoms should consult a doctor immediately. Gonorrhea can usually be treated by oral or intravenous medicines. If a man is not treated, he can continue to infect partners, and the untreated disease could lead to prostatitis, arthritis, heart disease, and skin infections.

The first symptom of syphilis is usually a chancre or ulcerated sore, which shows up on the sex organs or other parts of the exposed body in about three weeks after infection. At this early stage syphilis is curable—but highly contagious. If left untreated, syphilis can lead to damage of many parts of the body, including the brain, eyes, teeth, tongue, gums, heart, liver and kidneys, skin, joints, and legs.

How Drugs Affect Sexual Response

Tranquilizers, sedatives, and narcotics can cause partial or complete impotence. Men who take tranquilizers frequently suffer from ejaculatory incompetence (erection but not ejaculation—see Chapter VII), and persons addicted to barbiturates or opiates usually become impotent.

As we discussed in Chapter III, alcohol deadens sexual performance although it may increase desire. Even smoking may reduce potency by causing toxic changes in the blood that block the formation of sexual hormones. Dr. Magnus Hirschfeld, writing in *Sexual Pathology*, said: "I consider it quite certain that cigarette smokers, cigar smokers less, not rarely suffer injuries to their potency. There are cases in which a return to potency could be made possible merely through renouncing the use of cigarettes."

Some patients who have stopped cigarette smoking observed that their sexual drive increased markedly in the first several weeks, and some people have "regulated" their sexual lives by refraining from smoking when they wanted to increase their sexual drive.

Certain drugs that *may* heighten sexual response or excitement (or give the illusion of this) are amphetamines, benzedrine, cocaine, dexedrine, LSD, marijuana and hashish.

Drugs that usually repress the sex drive or lead to impotence are: Amytal/amobarbital/Amytal sodium (sedatives or "downers"), Demerol, Equanil, Heroin, Nembutal, opium.

Other drugs—including over-the-counter sleeping tablets—can affect sexual performance, especially if they are combined with alcohol (which increases their potency). Any prescription drug you might take could affect you in some way. If you're having problems and think it might be because of drugs you're taking, consult your doctor.

A word about caffeine. The Muslims called coffee the "black sheep of sleep and lovemaking." But its supposed effects on sex stem from the fact that the brew became popular in coffeehouses that were frequented by males. As men liked to swap stories and lies, argue politics and tell jokes, they preferred the coffeehouses as a refuge from the home. Their wives blamed coffee for their husbands' loss of interest in bed and board.

What the wives didn't know is that recent studies show that caffeine greatly increases the motility (spontaneous forward movement) of ejaculated sperm. The same laboratory tests also indicate that caffeine also increases the longevity of the spermatozoa, as judged by their activity.

How Your Environment Affects Your Sex Life

The people around you, the air your breathe, the radiation in the atmosphere, and the machinery you use may all affect your sexual activity. Here are some common problems:

Allergies. A husband may break out in hives every time he gets near his wife (or vice versa). Is he really allergic to her or to something she's wearing? In a case of a woman who had asthmatic attacks whenever her husband came near, doctors found that his shaving lotion was the cause. Eliminating the shaving lotion eliminated the allergy.

In another case, a husband had violent sneezing attacks every time he approached his wife. Doctors conducted allergy tests and pinpointed an allergy to vegetable gum. Unfortunately, the couple had to search for months before they found the agent: the wife's hair spray!

Approximately 10 percent of Americans have some sort of allergy, and this problem can affect where a couple lives, the type of furnishings they have, the types of food they eat, what they wear, and how they groom themselves—and whom they marry.

Unfortunately, allergies can't be cured, but a doctor can pinpoint the cause of an allergic reaction and often give the patient relief through injections.

Pollution. Allergic victims aren't the only ones suffering from air pollution. Laboratory studies have found that animals exposed to exhaust fumes developed illnesses, and many lost their desire to mate. Might not air pollution similarly affect the human sex drive?

Dr. Frank L. Rosen, addressing a recent convention of the American Medical Association, says that air pollution exacts a frightful price in the form of ill health and suffering, but he emphasized that there are few refuges from bad air, especially for the urban dweller.

Pollution may be caused by pollens, molds, and insecticide sprays. But the leader in self-created air pollution—smoking—is blamed for bronchial asthma, anginal pain, and lowered sex drive.

Radiation. We're all exposed to radiation, not only from medical X rays but from rocks, soil, outer space—and the fall-out from atomic and hydrogen devices.

Tests have shows that radiation causes animals and humans to age and die prematurely. In the 1930's—before science developed better protection against radiation—radiologists died at an average age of 55.8 years (with better protection, they now live to an average of 70.1 years). Survivors of the atomic bombing of Nagasaki, Japan, developed a high incidence of leukemia and aged prematurely.

Radiation damages the cell's code of life—DNA—causing mutation. This causes premature aging and shortens life, because the radiation distorts the normal transmission of DNA information within the nondividing cells, and from generation to generation in the dividing cells. Women of the Marshall Islands (who were exposed to fall-out from atomic bomb tests) had a high number of miscarriages and developed moles on their skin.

Among other chemical mutagens in the environment capable of causing DNA damage are drugs, pesticides, food additives, known cancer-producing compounds, and atmospheric pollution.

The answer: to prevent premature aging (and a lessened sex drive), choose an environment as free as possible from allergy-producing agents, air pollution, and radiation.

Some Machinery Can Alter Your Sex Drive

I thought the following item in the *Journal of the American Medical Association* was unusual until, in interviewing many doctors for this book, I found other variations of the same story. This particular case comes from Dr. Robert Zufall, Dover, New Jersey:

"Some time ago I treated a middle-aged man who arrived at the emergency room with multiple lacerations on his glans and penile shaft.

"He said that he had been in his backyard, clad only in his undershorts, and cleaning his car when the hand vacuum cleaner he was using became clogged with dirt and stopped.

"He sat down on his back steps, took the cleaner apart, and began to clean it out. Unfortunately, he had forgotten to turn it off; and, as he cleaned the last bit of debris that held the fan blades, the motor suddenly started, the penis was sucked into the whirring blades, and the damage was done."

The doctor said he was able to suture the cuts and they healed without incident, except for one cut which left the man with a deviated urinary stream. The doctor added: "I regarded the whole thing as somewhat apocryphal until, recently, I encountered another patient with an almost identical injury . . . so beware! It may be more common than you think!"

Doctors are almost unanimous in their belief that in all cases of illness and surgery, sexual activity should be resumed at the earliest possible moment consistent with the patient's health, to avoid unnecessary hardship and the risk of far-reaching effects on the marriage. They warn, however, about attempting sex too early (a failure might set a pattern for the future) or increasing activity just to prove you're as good as you were. One doctor concludes: "If a sexual attempt fails for any reason, the patient's frantic reaction may lead to more attempts, more failure, and possible sexual dysfunction."

In the next chapter we shall explore some new sexual techniques to bring added pleasure in later years, and how to "win" partners over to new practices.

IX
IT'S NEVER TOO LATE
TO TRY SOMETHING NEW

If sex is the ultimate communication, many of us have forgotten the language. It's not just words—it's looks, tones, actions, gestures, projections, assumptions, and expectations about sex.

Dr. Wardell Pomeroy, for years an associate of Dr. Alfred C. Kinsey, said recently: "If a husband and wife could only give each other hints and clues as to what excites them and how they feel about the kind of sex they have together, they could improve their relationship. Then, during the act itself, they should give vent to their feelings and express pleasure, so each partner would realize that the efforts are worthwhile."

How sad but true that after years of living and loving together most men and women don't really know (or care?) what pleases the other partner. None of us is so automatic in our appetites (eating or sex) that we want a steady steak diet—sometimes we might like hot dogs. Do you know what your partner wants every time ... does he/she know what you want? ... do you know what *you* really want?

Sexual arousal is physical and emotional. Each of us responds differently at different times. What "turns on" a person one time might "turn him off" another time. Unless the partners are keenly tuned to each other's needs and wants at the *moment*, they may be missing opportunities—or creating problems.

One marriage counselor tells of the woman whose marriage was falling apart because she always wanted to try a certain sex practice but was afraid her husband would think she was "perverted." The counselor persuaded the woman to ask her husband; he replied: "Sure, why didn't you ask before?" They tried it and didn't particularly like it, but went on to other sexual exploration that improved the marriage.

In the book *Sex Talk*, Myron Brenton lists these "sex risks" that people are reluctant to talk about:

● "deviations" such as oral sex; minor fetishes; more imaginative sex positions;

   ● more passive sex—masturbation rather than intercourse;

   ● more aggressive sex such as biting, scratching, moaning, screaming, using sex words, abandonment;

   ● a wish for emotional rather than physical satisfaction.

This last point applies especially to older couples. One wife complained that if she dared touch her spouse in the morning she was committing them to have sex that evening. Often all she wanted was just to *touch* her mate—not make love.

A husband complained that every time he attempted to touch his wife, put his arm around her, or take her hand, she pushed him away. The husband says he no longer can live in this "dead marriage" and wants to lead a more natural social and sexual life.

Babies who are deprived of touching, cuddling, and other signs of affection grow up to be frigid wives and impotent husbands. The same might be said of marriages. Any marriage that doesn't include touching, cuddling, or fondling—without any definite commitments—is frigid or impotent.

If men and women can learn to touch, hold, and stroke each other for those pleasures alone—*without committing themselves to sex*—then they will feel freer to signal for intercourse when *that* is their need.

Every marriage experiences a certain deteriorating loss of intimacy—less confiding, cuddling, kissing. But by maintaining contact through the sensitive nerve ending of the skin (tactile stimulation) the partners progress from *skin* love to *in* love. In this way, romance is a "touching" experience.

The fear or reluctance to touch, cuddle, or fondle often leads to a wife's developing a headache instead of affection; to a husband's working late instead of snuggling at home. If there's one thing the older generation could learn from the younger, it is that displays of affection—words, body contact, touching—are natural and normal forms of communication. Touching is especially sensitive communication because it transmits interest and tenderness.

Why Not Let It All Show?

Father Andrew Greeley, quoted earlier in this book, says that to be "sexy" we should create an erotic atmosphere of playfulness, challenge, and opportunity. It's not easy to do so if we're filled with fear, uncertainty, and shame. Shame is the enemy of sexiness— because of shame we may try to get sexual obligations over as quickly and routinely as possible, leaving little room or time for variety or playfulness. He may play the "tough guy" and she may play the "flirt," but they don't reveal their true selves. Comments Father Greeley: "A man who doesn't admit to a capacity for tenderness and sensitivity really isn't very sexy, and a woman who can't go beyond teasing to clear, direct, and vigorous passion appears erotic only to the shallowest and most superficial of partners." He calls for awareness of the body as an instrument of "erotic self-display."

Clothes are the most obvious forms of erotic display. But how sexy are tattered or dull-looking undergarments? One man complained that his wife's girdles had holes and her brassiere was fastened by a safety pin: "She cares a lot about how she looks to other people, but she doesn't give a damn about how she looks to me!" "Sexy" nightgowns and colorful panties, bras, and shorts can become erotic wrappings to be sensuously stripped from the package. Undressing then becomes the art of "stripteasing."

In the old days wives may have "bragged" that their husbands never saw them in the nude; they undressed in the bathroom, put on a nightgown, and made love beneath the blankets—with the light off. How much better to let *nothing* stand between you and your love. The feeling of skin upon skin is also an ultimate form of sexual communication.

Other Barriers to Sexual Exploring

Dr. James Leslie McCary, a member of the psychology department at the University of Houston, Texas, says: "The middle-aged husband may be blessed with a sexual partner who has not only overcome many or most of her sexual inhibitions with the passage of time and growing maturity, but who also has stronger sexual needs than ever before. She is therefore much more likely than a younger wife to be willing—even eager—to initiate sexual interaction with her husband and to provide whatever stimulation and excitement her husband may wish."

Dr. Abraham Maslow identified the most orgasmic women as those who were not passive, submissive, or conventionally feminine. New York psychotherapist Dr. Judith Antrobus says: "I find many men who report they feel more, rather than less, potent with women who make their sexual interests and enthusiasms known."

Perhaps the reluctance of some women to express themselves stems from the fact that as little girls they were taught that sex is something you do to please your husband. They didn't even discover their own sensuality—the clitoris as their course of erotic pleasure—unless by accidental exploring. Then if they were caught masturbating, they were admonished: "Nice little girls don't do that." On the other hand, boys were taught early that it's "manly" to "score" with a girl, and they started playing the "numbers game." Equating quantity with quality doesn't allow time to learn the rules of the game, however, and they eventually lose, no matter how often they "score."

Unfortunately, the man is supposed to be the "teacher" in many marriages, and his own ignorance—and pressure to measure up to some mythical "standard" of sexual frequency—often leads to frustration and failure for both partners. If the husband expects the wife to be passive she will be—putting even more pressure on him to produce the magical orgasm. When he fails (probably from trying too hard) and she fails (because she's too passive), the marriage is in trouble.

Masters and Johnson recognize the dominant/submissive problems in most marriages, which is why they use male/female therapy teams for couples to identify with. Mrs. Johnson notes that nine out of every ten wives are unable to tell their husbands which stimulation they prefer in bed. Through "show and tell" sessions the therapists try to get the couple to cooperate as sexual partners.

The Long and Short of Penis Size

Concern over penis size may block some sexual exploration. Most doctors agree, however, that the size of a penis doesn't matter in a happy marriage. The "average" erect male penis is between 5½ and 6½ inches. Most sexologists believe that the vagina can easily accommodate an erect organ within 4 to 7 inches. Some women may have trouble adapting to penises shorter than 4 inches or longer than 7 inches (erect). Different positions, however, alter vagina shape and depth so that it can adjust to almost any penis size. For example, the rear entry position provides a snugger, more stimulating fit for a small penis. And by keeping her legs together in the male-on-top position, the woman prevents full penetration of an exceptionally long penis.

Actually, penis size makes little difference. Studies show that small penises expand to twice their size and larger penises expand much less, so that the erect smaller penis is generally big enough for sexual intercourse. Also, it is not necessary for a woman to experience internal stimulation to reach orgasm. The vagina interior is *not* heavily supplied with sensitive nerve endings; the woman's most erotic organs—the clitoris and vaginal lips—are outside the vaginal tube.

Thus, most women couldn't care less about penis size. If they're emotionally involved with their partner they are more concerned with his warmth, consideration, understanding, and personality than they are with his small or large penis.

Crank Up the Emotions—and the Motions

Dr. Albert Ellis asks us to *think*—concentrate—on sex. He says: "If you deliberately concentrate on heightening your sensations and feelings while you are going through love play, you'll usually find pleasures that you were hardly aware of. Rather than just letting sex joy occur, you can often make it occur—if you really try to feel it and enhance it."

Another sexologist describes sex as "bodies in motion and glands in commotion." First things first. Before bodies get in motion, the glands must be put in commotion. And it's not a "push-button" job.

Dr. Joseph H. Peck, author of *All About Men,* compares a man's arousal to a woman's by comparing a modern Cadillac with a Model T Ford. He says the man is like the Cadillac—quick starts and high speed—but "minus the brakes and helpless if the starter fails to work." He then describes the woman's arousal like that of a Model T Ford. It takes a lot of patience, manpower, and proper timing to crank her up, but once she gets going, she's more likely to get there. He adds: "A slow warm-up, with particular attention to every detail, and yours will be a happy household . . . but if you are remiss in this duty, better prepare for trouble."

Older men should have the time, patience, wisdom, and experience for a slow warm-up. The fact that the man may be slower in sexual arousal helps slow the process for the benefit of both.

Timing is important in more ways than one. Dr. McCary says that sex among older couples is characteristically a predictable, brief encounter that probably follows a Saturday-night party at which all drank intemperately. In such relationships, wives frequently describe their sex life as "legal prostitution, not much better than masturbation"; and their husbands refer to their spouses as "legal, inexpensive, clean mechanisms for physical gratification."

Instead of making sex something you do after a party or the 11 o'clock news, why not make it something you do when you feel like it—maybe before dinner and after a couple of relaxing drinks. Some couples have the gift of telling each other what they want—when they want it. If they don't communicate by words, they do so by provoking, tantalizing, stimulating—imaginative play that creates its own excitement. The game communicates to each partner: "You guess what will please me and I'll guess what will please you."

Lack of communication often signifies inhibition. Researchers at the Center for Marital and Sexual Studies in Long Beach, California, found that couples who volunteer to have sex while being clinically measured and observed are very quiet while making love. The researchers postulate that the vast majority of inhibited persons are usually silent during the sex act.

Many people might like to scream, groan, cry out, or utter sex words—but they stifle the impulse. These signals can tell your partner how things are going and can guide him/her to what's best for both of you. The more we bottle up our feelings, the more inhibited and awkward we become in using the language of sex under any circumstances.

Communicating by Touch and Caress

The type of touch, caress, or embrace carries its own message. Dr. Josef E. Garai, professor of psychology at the School of Humanities and Social Science, Pratt Institute, New York, says: "When you are tired or not in the mood for intercourse, a loving, lasting embrace may be all that's needed to gain what good sex gives; the warmth and life-pulsating force of the partner, a sense of deep security and true contentment."

However, when you want to communicate (stimulate) sexual response in your partner, you should have a pretty good idea of what you're doing and where you're going.

If you want to stimulate someone sexually, you'll caress and touch the erogenous zones—those places containing masses of tiny nerve endings near the surface. They are located around body openings; besides the genital areas, sensitive areas include the skin around the anus, mouth, nose, and ears. Also sensitive are the inner thighs, the neck, parts of the back, and the knees.

Those who "kiss and tell" say they prefer (in order) lips, tongue, breasts, genitals. Those who "touch and tell" say they prefer breasts (female), then genitals.

But, remember, the same person may respond differently at different times, so vary your routes to erotic happiness.

Under usual circumstances, a woman likes to have her breasts—especially the nipples—properly stimulated. Using his tongue, penis (tip or glans), or hand, a man can stimulate round and round the nipple, then softly knead the breast with both hands, or gently bite or suck. Stimulation traps blood, and it's not uncommon for an "aroused" breast to swell 20 to 25 percent, exposing more areas and nerve endings to stimulation.

Before the whole breast enlarges, the nipple usually responds. In fact, it's so sensitive it can become erect even through changes in temperature. In some senses, the nipples are too responsive, and continued stimulation may eventually produce irritation. However, the swelling areolae (area surrounding the nipples) become firm and act as a moderating cushion to protect and transmit sensations to the nipples.

A man can stimulate the breasts by massaging them (sometimes with lubricating jelly). Perhaps 2 percent or more of women can reach orgasm through breast manipulation alone. One woman says she has orgasm when her partner stimulates the nipple with his penis tip until he ejaculates. She says the breast orgasm is as good as a coital one—she feels it inside. She says breast orgasms from licking and handling are "in between" in feeling.

Another woman says: "Men still don't understand about breasts, or are in too much of a hurry to get lower down. Unlike a man's nipples, a woman's have a direct hot line to her clitoris. A man who can dial this correctly and will only take the time can do anything." (Remember, though, sex stimulation isn't push-button manipulation.)

The clitoris also receives stimulation from other parts of the body, and it has its own dynamic set of sensitive nerves. It receives stimulation from the vulva (the external sex organs) and from the lips of the vagina. The clitoris looks something like a raised tunnel, which widens as it descends from its origin at the upper meeting point of the major lips. At the mouth of this shaft is a small rounded body, about the size of a pea, that forms the most sensitive glans part of the clitoris.

The clitoris, unlike any male organ, has only one purpose— sexual stimulation. But when the clitoris has passed through its first phase of stimulation, it responds to greater stimulation by drawing up, not by extending downward. Thus, in excitement the clitoris is less exposed and more protected (somewhat like the nipple). As the clitoris withdraws when a woman is sexually aroused, it is practically impossible to make direct contact with it in intercourse. But as the male organ thrusts in and out, it exerts some friction to the minor lips of the vagina. These lips are linked to the clitoris. Any stimulation around the clitoris—especially the lips and hood surrounding it—transmits sensation and can cause orgasm.

Because of its extreme sensitivity, direct stimulation of the clitoris must be light. Rough handling will cause pain rather than pleasure, and may turn off the orgasm.

The erogenous zones of the male are more limited, and his sexual arousal is more direct. One reason is that to preserve the race, man must reach ejaculation; a woman need not reach orgasm. This explains, in part, why men are so genital-oriented and may bypass other female erogenous zones.

Besides the genitals, other male erogenous zones may be the earlobes and the nipples—which also become erect during sexual excitement. A talented female can also train a man to respond to skin sensitivity, but the fact remains that most—though not all—male feeling is centered in the last inch of the penis.

Most men get their greatest pleasure when the woman fondles the penis head, strokes the shaft, and stimulates the glans (near the penis head) with the tip of a finger or the tongue. Penis stimulation sends nerve impulses to the sexual center in the spinal cord. At a peak of stimulation, a reflex action takes place in this center, commanding the muscles involved in ejaculation to contract.

As in the female, stimulation causes blood to become trapped and the sex organ to become larger and firmer. Sensitive nerve areas are expanded and exposed to greater sensitivity. As the skin stretches, it exposes more surface to stimulation; and as the stiffened organ offers increased resistance to pressure, the male feels touch more keenly.

A man's testicles are also sensitive to touch—but gently, gently.

Are There Really Different Types of Orgasm?

Orgasm means different things to different women. For some women it can be extreme ecstasy, for others, a mere emotional ripple. Some say they feel a clitoral orgasm more intensely but a vaginal one more fully.

According to Dr. Harvey L. Resnik, a psychoanalyst of Chevy Chase, Maryland, the physiologic response is the same whether orgasm occurs through stimulation of the clitoris alone or through deep penetration. The differences between orgasms are the result rather of other circumstances, such as mood, level of fatigue, and expectation, which affect body responses.

Doctors describe the female orgasm as a series of rhythmic

reflex contractions of the muscles surrounding the vagina. Like other reflexes—a sneeze or blinking of the eye—various stimuli can trigger orgasm. In a really good orgasm, the woman doesn't know where she is or how she got there. But some women have a low orgasmic threshold and others have a high one; both may be perfectly normal.

A noted sexologist, P. H. Gebhard, suggests that the female's ability to reach orgasm is closely related to the length of both foreplay and intromission. His studies showed that three-fifths of women always reach orgasm if foreplay lasts longer than twenty minutes, and half reach orgasm after fifteen to twenty minutes of foreplay. Gebhard concluded that intromission of less than one minute was too brief to permit most women to reach orgasm, that intromission of one to eleven minutes would bring about half of all women to orgasm, and that intromission lasting more than sixteen minutes would bring all women "to the limits of their orgasmic capacities."

Since Kinsey and other researchers found that three out of four men reach orgasm in less than two minutes after entry and many within ten to twenty seconds, the male is the obvious cause of much female inadequacy. About 10 to 15 percent of married women never achieve orgasm during coitus, and about 40 percent achieve it virtually every time. That still leaves a large percentage of unsatisfied women.

In *The Key to Feminine Response in Marriage*, Ronald M. Deutsch writes: "In the art of love, there is a good parallel in the behavior of the true gourmet. His attention is devoted to bringing all his senses to bear upon the fullest appreciation of what is before him. He does not wolf his meal while thinking only of his after-dinner cigar. The senses belong to the very immediate and poignant present. The psychological blocks to physical love operate precisely by intruding upon the present the anger and hurt of the past and the fear of the future."

Some men adopt a "stop-start" pattern of pleasure. They reach a certain peak, withdraw, lose the erection, and start over again. Dr. Arnold A. Lazarus, Yale University, says this pattern is based on the fact that, as intercourse begins, both partners usually feel an initial surge of eroticism. As intercourse continues they reach a "pleasure plateau" before climax. If they stop while they are on that plateau, simmer down, then climb back up again, they can prolong their enjoyment innumerable times—and the female usually has a series of orgasms. When they finally reach climax, it's a violent one, as they have climbed higher and higher erotic levels together.

Simultaneous Orgasm: Nice, But Necessary?

As you know, a woman can have multiple orgasms, whereas a man has only one and then needs a rest before another climax. Thus, it is logical that a woman should have several orgasms before the man has his "grand finale."

Dr. Joseph E. Garai says: "All the talk we hear about the joys of a simultaneous orgasm can make us forget our separate individualities. 'Merging into oneness' is merely an illusion; soon after the sexual act we return to our separate spaces and existences . . . it is time to realize that people can have a relationship in which they 'come together' without also being 'stuck together.' "

He illustrates this with a poem:

"She said to him with a pleasant smile;
'Let's try to come together once in a while! . . .
But people who are genuinely relaxed and smart
Will sometimes come together and sometimes apart.' "

Dr. Harold Lear, a urologist at Mt. Sinai Hospital, New York, adds: "Everything's relative. If a wife comes in thirty-five seconds, it doesn't matter if the man comes in forty-five—unless it's a problem to them. On the one hand, they may be having the greatest sex life together. On the other, it might be one of the great tragedies of their lives."

While a woman may have another orgasm in a few seconds, after a man has his one "big shot" he needs a rest before another ejaculation—lasting from two minutes to twenty-four hours.

How long should couples wait between simultaneous orgams? That depends upon the state of energy and general health. But Dr. Lazarus says that the "optimal deprivation" (the correct amount of time you should abstain from a new round of sex in order to make sure your orgasm will be as strong as possible) usually means not having sex from eight to forty-eight hours after one's last intercourse.

What's the Best Position for Maximum Pleasure?

The six basic positions (allowing for infinite variations) are: (1) man on top; (2) woman on top; (3) sitting; (4) standing; (5) side-by-side; and (6) penetration from the rear.

About 70 percent of our society seems to feel that the "man on top" is the "superior" position. However, the amused natives of the South Pacific called this the "missionary position." And a study by the late Clyde Kluckhohn, a Harvard anthropologist, of favored coital positions in 193 cultures found that the commonest method of copulation was insertion from the rear, with the male squatting behind the female.

One problem with the "male on top" is that it increases stimulation in the male, and may induce him to reach orgasm too soon. Also, the man must support his weight on his legs, arms, and hands and thus is not able to caress the woman or pause very long to slow down his response.

Men who insist on the "missionary position" may do so because they feel that they have to be in full control of the situation, including the timing of *their* ejaculation (but not of the female's orgasm).

They may be among those who think the "female on top" is a "depraved reversal" of the customary position. They might be interested to know that thousands of friezes and drawings depicting coitus dating back to 3000 B.C. in Mesopotamia, Egypt, India, China, and Peru show the female in the "superior" position. It was so conventional that references to other procedures in heterosexual intercourse were found mainly in pornography.

The female superior position allows the woman greater movement and frees the male's hands for caressing. It also allows the woman to control the movements for her greater pleasure and to regulate the male's ejaculation.

Friction overstimulates the man but masks sensations in the woman. Vigorous friction as soon as the male enters almost assures blurred sensation and declining sexual tension. Better a slow rotary motion of the hips, circular or forward-backward, to stimulate the vaginal walls and take pressure from the end. By leaning all the way forward and pressing against the man, the woman can reduce the movement of the penis and slow the man"s response, while stimulating her clitoris. As she nears orgasm, she can raise her hips and allow the man to set the pace to his own response.

For additional female stimulation, the man sits upright, with his legs separated, and the woman sits between his legs with her back against his chest and her legs separated and thrown over his. Her genital region is exposed, and he is in a good position to stimulate her wherever she desires.

Another variation of the female superior position is for the woman to lie partly above the man, with her head beside his, with her lower leg extending between his legs, and her upper leg over his upper one. His lower leg is bent at the knee, flat on the bed to cradle her as they face each other. This position offers the greatest control of male ejaculation. He can stop at any time, and the woman has freedom of movement.

Another "major" position is the rear entry, which the Greeks and Romans thought was the most natural. In this the man kneels or lies behind the woman, and the penis enters the vagina from below her buttocks. The partners may lie side by side, with the man leaning slightly backward and curving his pubic region under hers. The partners may also kneel, with the man's hips being lowered beneath the woman's buttocks. Or they may kneel with the woman resting her chest on her knees and her head on the bed, and the man kneeling behind her in an upright "knee-chest" position. Although this position offers little or no clitoral contact and limited penetration, many sexologists say that women who reach orgasm in other positions can also reach orgasm in this manner.

Several standing and sitting positions also offer variety. In the simplest sitting position, the man sits on a chair or bed, and the woman faces him and lowers herself, sitting high on his flanks. There is maximum clitoral pressure, the penis is fully caressed, the woman can control the movements and degree of arousal, and each partner is free to caress the other.

Sometimes changing positions improves performance. Dr. Hugo G. Beigel, personal consultant, tells of one woman who hated intercourse because the man's weight threatened to suffocate her. She was small and fragile, and he was big and heavy, yet they only engaged in the man-on-top position. Dr. Beigel recommended that they try either the woman-on-top or the rear-entry position. They took his advice; for the first time in their marriage they both enjoyed intercourse.

Most counselors say that any position that is comfortable and allows greatest freedom of movement (especially for the woman) is proper. Once intercourse begins, it requires active behavior of both partners to please each other and themselves. Sexologists also note that the shallow thrust during the early part of intercourse tends to tease a woman, thus adding to her desire.

The Exercise That Improves Pleasure and Performance

In Chapter V we mentioned the Kegel exercise that strengthens the pelvic muscles and heightens sexual satisfaction. The particular muscle strengthened is the *pubococcygeus*, commonly abbreviated as

P.C. This muscle runs from the pubis, the bony prominence at the front of the pelvis, to the coccyx, the end of the spine.

In stress incontinence, the sphincteric action of that part of the P.C. surrounding the urinary passage fails. But exercise can strengthen it enough to control the urine flow.

At first the Kegel exercise was used only for urinary control, until women noticed an interesting side benefit—it increased sexual pleasure for themselves as well as their mates. One reason is that the P.C. muscle can narrow the vagina to a tight, firm channel, which increases stimulation for both men and women. The stimulated muscle will automatically contract, helping build tension that leads to the female climax.

Dr. Arnold H. Kegel developed a simple way in which most women can do this exercise. Remember that, among other functions, the P.C. controls urinary flow. However, since weaker external muscles also shut off urine, these must be kept out of play. To do so, the woman separates her knees widely; once urine begins to flow she squeezes the P.C. muscles to stop it.

Once women learn the sensation of P.C. contraction, most of them can repeat the contraction at any time, anywhere, using urinary control only as a check. Women can begin the exercise with five or ten contractions before arising in the morning, and repeat perhaps at six intervals during the day. As each contraction takes no more than a second, this requires only one minute a day.

Dr. Kegel suggests that women use each urination to practice the exercise. She can easily step up the contractions to 300 a day with no effort. After about six to eight weeks a woman can stop the exercise, as the normal P.C. muscle stays partially contracted. Also, sexual activity helps preserve the new muscle tone.

A Little Spice May Make Things Nice

Some persons believe "perversion" is any deviation from male-over-female or female-over-male in anything other than vaginal intercourse.

But, as we have noted before, most doctors and sexologists believe that *anything goes* as long as both partners agree to the practice and like it. It becomes abnormal only when one person wants it and the other doesn't.

In *Sex Talk*, Myron Brenton suggests that when one person wants to try something but the other partner is reluctant, both should try to generate a free and open atmosphere to express themselves. Sometimes this exploration leads the reluctant person to change his/her attitudes because of realizing, "I don't have to feel guilty about doing this."

If the partners reach an impasse, Brenton suggests that the willing partner can: (1) force the reluctant partner; (2) nourish a grudge; (3) seek someone else to have the pleasure with; or (4) evaluate the situation in terms of the overall relationship.

If the overall relationship is more important than the transitory pleasure, then he/she can let the matter drop. But if the willing person still has longings, he/she can ask these questions: "What does this really mean to me, aside from erotic pleasure? Am I involved in a power struggle? Does the technique have a special significance to me that I haven't fully acknowledged or recognized?" If you're honest with yourself, you'll discover something new. And this discovery may lessen the need for the technique in question. Sexual "games" may merely satisfy perverse feelings such as hate, spite, anger, fear, guilt, shame, or other hang-ups.

What Are Some Common Sexual Variations?

Oral-Genital Sex. Many people are hung-up on mouth-to-genital contact because their early religious training said it was sinful. Interestingly enough, cultures outside the Judeo-Christian consider this practice perfectly acceptable, and museums in the Middle East and in South America exhibit terra-cotta sculptures and paintings of people in all kinds of sexual engagement, including oral-genital.

According to the Kinsey-Pomeroy reports about a generation ago, some 60 percent of the participants had had oral-genital experience before marriage, and it was assumed that married couples would engage in oral-genital sex even more. Further studies show that mouth-genital contacts are increasing, particularly among persons in the higher socioeconomic groups.

Sexologists say that people in love desire to share their lives and bodies as completely as possible; therefore it's perfectly natural for them to want to touch, caress, and kiss any part of a mate's body, including the genital area.

When a woman orally stimulates the penis it's called *fellatio*—licking and flicking the penis head and shaft with the tongue and tongue tip, and taking the penis into the mouth and sucking on it.

When the man orally stimulates the clitoris and vagina, it's called *cunnilingus*—sucking the clitoris with the lips, licking or flicking it with the tongue or tongue-tip, licking the vaginal ridge, sucking the genital-lips with the mouth-lips, and inserting the tongue into the vagina.

Dr. Robert Chartham, author of *The Sensuous Couple,* says that fellatio is not just a matter of putting the penis-head into the mouth and sucking it. He says the fellator must know the sensitive areas of the penis (in descending order of sensitivity): the frenum (underneath the tip), the rim (both around the edge and in the groove under it), the base of the penis all around, about an inch and a half above the root, the whole length of the underside of the shaft, and, finally, the rest of the skin of the penis.

The fellator must never bite the penis, and she must draw her lips down and under (or over) the edges of her teeth to protect the penis.

The woman will know when the man is about to ejaculate; he will begin to breathe heavily and his testes will rise and lower more frequently. Some women are willing to let the man ejaculate in their mouths and swallow the semen. Doctors say this is harmless, as semen is mainly made up of salts and vitamins.

Dr. Chartham says that cunnilingus is also an art. The man can begin by using his tongue-tip to run around the rim of the vaginal entrance, then gradually sliding the flat of his tongue up the vaginal ridge until he reaches the clitoris.

He can then vary his caresses by licking the clitoral area with the flat of his tongue, teasing the clitoris-head with rapid flicks of the tongue-tip, or taking the clitoris head between his lips and sucking strongly on it. He can alternate by inserting his tongue penislike in the vagina, and going back and forth between the vagina and clitoris until the woman breathes heavily and is reaching climax. At this point the clitoris will retreat back into its hood, and the man can complete the orgasm for both of them by inserting his penis in her vagina and finishing off with strong strokes.

Dr. Chartham adds that, with practice, couples should be able to have simultaneous cunnilingus and fellatio. He adds that it would be wise for each couple to wash their genitals before performing oral sex; however, vigorous sexual intercourse will usually make the odors right.

Whatever form of love-making you use, remember that the postcoital, or afterplay, is an important part of the communication. In many instances, a woman doesn't have the immediate release that a man has, and she's still on a high emotional plateau. During afterplay she likes to be held in her lover's arms, to feel close to him, to feel wanted and loved, not just desired. This, too, is the communication of love.

In the next chapter we shall examine some visual stimuli— notably pornography—and what effects they might have on sexual arousal and lovemaking.

X
PORNOGRAPHY –
OR GOOD CLEAN FUN?

When Gertrude Stein was on her deathbed, she murmured: "What's the answer?" The assembled friends were silent, so Miss Stein whispered: "Then, what's the question?"

Perhaps this clarifies as much as possible the situation concerning pornography and obscenity in America today—there are as many questions as there are answers.

First some definitions:

Obscenity stems from the Latin *obscaenus,* meaning "adverse, inauspicious, ill-omened." Today, obscenity means "indecency, lewdness, or offensiveness in behavior, expression, or appearance."

Pornography stems from the Greek *pornographos,* meaning "writing about prostitutes." Today, pornography means "written, graphic, or other forms of communication intended to excite lascivious feelings."

Given the ancient origins of these words, it is obvious that obscenity and pornography have been around a long time. Why? Everybody gets something out of it. The producers get rich on little risk, the participants supposedly have "fun," the purchasers get "thrills," and the crusaders have a moral cause.

Even the respected artists of past eras manipulated pornography. During the eighteenth century some of the most eminent writers in France—Voltaire, the Baron de Montesquieu, Denis Diderot, Jean Jacques Rousseau, Restif de la Bretonne, Julien Offroy de la Mettrie—made lots of money writing pornography.

One of the best works—*Les Liaisons Dangereuses*—traced the degeneracy of two aristocratic libertines who maliciously ruined other people, and eventually themselves, through sadism, perversions, and sexual excesses. The work actually was moralistic, underscoring the difference between good and evil, but it was read mainly for its purple passages of the corruption in the court of Louis XVI.

153

What Is the State of the "Art" Today?

To paraphrase a commercial, "We've come a long way, baby!" From crudely drawn "comic books" depicting sexual activity, we've blossomed into slick, microscopically detailed colored photographs of everything you've always wanted to see about sex (but didn't know existed?). From poorly plotted, silent, and grainy "stag films" we've developed complexly plotted sound and color, artistically filmed "Super-X"-rated films that boggle mind and body.

Basically, here's the situation today:

Movies Are Better Than Ever? General-release films are getting sexier. Themes now include adultery, promiscuity, abortion, perversion, spouse-swapping, orgies, male and female homosexuality, etc. Graphically, the films depict partial and complete nudity, and the sexual activity simulates, suggests, or even depicts intercourse, masturbation, fellatio, and cunnilingus.

In short, general-release movies are now where the "art films" were in the 1950's and 1960's. Today, only their "foreignness" or limited audience appeal sets art films apart from general-release movies.

For even more explicit sex, the big trend is toward "skin flicks." These low budget films (perhaps only $50,000) show at relatively fewer theaters (however, only "family" theaters are now exempt), and themes and graphics leave nothing to the imagination.

Books and Magazines: "Show and Tell?" All general books and magazines tell and show more sex. In fact, magazines such as *Playboy, Penthouse, Oui,* and *Viva,* depicting total nudity and detailing sexual activity, might be classified as "general" magazines today.

The "secondary" or "adults only" market also flourishes. "Adults only" paperback books range from "sex pulp" books (stories of sexual misadventures with minimal plot and basic language) to explicit "marriage manuals." Most "adults only" books aim at heterosexual males, but more and more seek to satisfy the appetites of homosexuals, lesbians, and fetishists.

The "adults only" magazines spare words but stress graphics, including color closeups of "straight" and anal intercourse, fellatio, cunnilingus, homosexuality, lesbianism, fetishes, sadomasochism (bondage, chains, whips, spanking, rubber and leather wearing apparel, high-heeled boots, etc.)—in singles, doubles, triples, and "casts of thousands."

As it costs more to produce these magazines and paperback books and the runs are limited, they usually cost from $2.50 to $5 each.

The Things They Send Through the Mails! Mail-order operators offer varied sexually oriented materials to satisfy every taste. Most popular are heterosexually oriented magazines, books, 8 mm movies, sexual devices, and advertisements for "swinger" clubs. Operators aim about 10 percent of their material at homosexuals and a smaller amount at fetishists.

Most houses mail to a solicited list (the person requested it), or a semisolicited list (the mailer got it from another mailer in the same business). Mailers sometimes "shotgun" mailings to people who didn't request them, and these are the people who usually complain about erotica in the mails.

The "Hard" Stuff You Get "Under the Counter." "Hard-core" pornography generally confines itself to photographic reproductions of vaginal, anal, or oral intercourse. You can buy it in three forms: motion pictures ("stag films"), photo sets, and picture magazines. Although the stag-film market may be declining (you can see them at local theaters), the picture magazines are booming. At first these magazines were imported from more "liberated" countries such as Denmark, but local productions now flourish.

Who Likes and Buys the Stuff?

At some point, approximately 85 percent of adult men and 70 percent of adult women in America see some pornography. What they see generally follows their sexual interest: heterosexual intercourse, some homosexuality and oral sex; less sadomasochistic sexual activity.

People who have higher educations and are more socially and politically active see the most erotic literature; those who attend religious services the least.

Reports indicate that between one-quarter and one-half the people who see explicit sexual material buy it, and many people share it—usually with a friend of the same sex or with a spouse.

A recent survey of patrons of adult movies and adult bookstores concluded that the "typical" patrons were "predominantly white, middle-class, middle-aged, married males, dressed in business suit or neat casual attire, shopping or attending the movie alone."

In a study of 5,000 customers of adult movie theaters in nine different communities, about 41 percent were estimated to be between the ages forty and sixty and 10 percent over age sixty. Eighty percent were white, 14 percent black, 5 percent Spanish-American, and 2 percent Oriental. Ninety-eight percent were male; the 2 percent of females mainly patronized suburban locations, and all were with a male escort or in a mixed group. Ninety percent of the males attended alone. Twenty-nine percent were estimated to be lower class, 53 percent middle class, and 16 percent upper middle class.

On the basis of these studies, the typical patron of adult movie theaters fits that general pattern of a predominantly white, middle-class, middle-age, married male who attends alone. The same general statistics apply to patrons of arcades or "peep shows."

How Do "Sexy" Materials Affect You?

When questioned about the erotic effects of a particular film, most persons said they were more *desirable* than undesirable. Over half said they learned something from the film and that they "fantasized" (humorously or sexually) about the picture. Almost half mentioned the film's social value, and approximately one-quarter referred to its sexual stimulus.

Another survey found that patrons of adult movies generally lead active and varied sex lives. Almost all have a regular partner, most have intercourse twice a week or more, and most report having had intercourse with more than one person during the past year. Most report that the films motivate them to introduce variety into their sexual lives.

Buyers of erotic material tend to report that their parents were somewhat permissive regarding nudity and erotic materials.

Recent research points out that *women are about as aroused as men when viewing sexual materials.* In responses to two erotic films, almost 80 percent of the males reported partial erection and 20 percent reported full erection lasting at least three minutes. Eighty-five percent of the females reported mild to strong genital sensations; others reported breast sensations and vaginal lubrication, and one reported having orgasm!

Research also shows that those who are college educated, religiously inactive, and sexually experienced are more likely to be aroused than persons who are less educated, religiously active, and sexually inexperienced.

What Scenes and Themes Turn You On?

Studies at the University of Hamburg Institute of Sex Research (confirmed by American studies) show that films and pictures depicting heterosexual activity (petting, coitus, oral sexuality) aroused 86 percent of the male viewers and 65 percent of the female.

But more males than females report arousal to oral sexuality, whereas females report more and stronger genital responses to films depicting sexual intercourse.

To test sexual themes, researchers provided subjects with 700-word stories divided into "realistic" and "hard core" (more fantasy). They found that males and females didn't differ significantly in the extent to which they judged erotically "realistic" stories as sexually stimulating, but females judged "hard-core" stories as much more stimulating than did males.

Regardless of the medium, both men and women were "turned on" by cunnilingus, "straight" intercourse, fellatio, female masturbation, nude heterosexual petting, and rear-entry intercourse. They were least aroused by male nudity, "female torturing male," and homosexual anal intercourse. Males like group oral sex more than females, and females liked homosexual fellatio and male masturbation better than males.

One study continuously exposed erotic materials to couples. After fifteen days, they reached a saturation point and were only partially rejuvenated by novel sex stimuli. But they partially recovered their interest after two months of nonexposure.

What Are the More Lasting Effects on Sexual Behavior?

When exposed to erotic materials, some persons increase their masturbation or heterosexual activities, but most remain about the same. Any sexual increases generally disappear within forty-eight hours. When masturbation follows (or accompanies) exposure, it usually occurs in persons who regularly masturbate or who have established but unavailable partners. When sexual intercourse increases following sexual stimuli, it generally occurs among sexually experienced persons with willing and available sexual partners. In one study, middle-aged married couples reported having more and varied sex during the twenty-four hours after viewing erotic films.

In general, after exposure to erotic stimuli, viewers didn't alter established sexual patterns. When sexual activity followed viewing or reading materials, it usually followed existing patterns.

Two studies found that after viewing erotic materials, most couples found it easier to talk about sexual matters. One study found that after exposure persons became more tolerant of other persons' sexual activities, although their own sexual standards didn't change.

Do erotic materials increase sex crimes? Sex-crime rates in

Denmark indicate that the more available are sex materials, the fewer the sex crimes. Research also indicates that sex offenders have seen *less* erotic material during earlier years. This early inexperience may even have led them to commit the sex crime.

To test *your* reaction to sexy books or films, Myron Brenton, author of *Sex Talk*, suggests you ask yourself these questions:

1. Did the book or movie offend, disgust, amuse, excite, or bore you?

2. Was there any part that particularly turned you on?

3. Any part that particularly turned you off?

4. Any part that reminded you of something about yourself you'd rather not have been reminded of?

5. Any part that made you very angry?

6. Any part that made you want to try it?

7. Any character you'd like to have been or played?

If you can answer these questions honestly, your reactions may surprise you—but you'll learn a lot about yourself.

What Does the Public Think About Pornography?

In 1967 Congress created a commission to "investigate the effects of pornography and obscenity on the people of the United States." Congress asked the commission to address itself to a "matter of national concern." Yet when the commission questioned people about their concerns of the day, 54 percent cited the war in Vietnam; 36 percent were primarily worried about racial conflict; 32 percent were concerned about inflation, taxation, and unemployment; 19 percent about pollution; and 4 percent about education. This left only 2 percent who were at all "concerned" about pornography, which led to one conclusion of the commission: "We find it [pornography] a nuisance rather than an evil, and the American public apparently agrees."

As to how divided the nation is on the subject of obscenity and pornography, the commission stated: "Public opinion in America does not support the imposition of legal prohibitions upon the rights of adults to read or see explicitly sexual materials."

One dissenting commissioner, Charles H. Keating, Jr., founder of Citizens for Decent Literature, Cincinnati, Ohio, took an opposing view: "Credit the American public with enough common sense to know that one who wallows in filth is going to get dirty. This is intuitive knowledge. Those who spend millions of dollars to tell us otherwise must be malicious or misguided or both."

And two other commissioners, the Rev. Morton A. Hill, S.J., president of Morality in Media, New York, and the Rev. Winfrey C. Link, administrator of the McKendree Manor Methodist Retirement Home, Hermitage, Tennessee, stated their minority opinion with these striking words: "The Commission's majority report is a Magna Carta for the pornographer."

Twelve of the eighteen members voted for the commission's basic recommendation: "Federal, state, and local legislation prohibiting the sale, exhibition, and distribution of sexual material to consenting adults should be repealed." Five other commissioners dissented, and one abstained.

The commission's majority view also implies that obscenity, like beauty, is in the eye of the beholder, and it recommended launching a massive sex-education effort. It also called for continued open discussion, based on factual information, on the issues regarding obscenity and pornography . . . "that citizens organize themselves at local, regional, and national levels to aid in the implementation of the foregoing recommendations."

The commission also made legislative recommendations that have been largely ignored by recent Supreme Court actions, although the commission's report may yet become a yardstick for contemporary community standards.

Where Do the Courts Stand?

The First Amendment to the United States Constitution prohibits the local, state, and national governments from passing any laws abridging freedom of speech and the press. More specifically, the ruling seems to say: You can freely discuss matters relating to sex and you can privately possess pornography . . . you can't participate in distributing "hard-core pornography," but it's hard to determine what materials fall under this definition.

However, recent decisions of the Supreme Court have established what Chief Justice Warren Burger calls "concrete guidelines for states wanting to ban obscene books, movies, and magazines."

Already some states have acted. The local school board of Drake, North Dakota, burned three dozen copies of Kurt Vonnegut's now famous and well-regarded book, *Slaughterhouse-Five*. The story brings to mind Franklin D. Roosevelt, who signed the first proclamation reducing postage rates on books in the 1930's, saying: "Here is the difference between Nazism and democracy. They are burning books, while we here are going to make them as available as possible."

Maybe not quite. Although current polls show that the majority of Americans believe they should decide what they may see and hear, recent Supreme Court decisions indicate you may do as you please with your body, but your eyes and ears are restricted.

One commentator says the situation relating to obscenity today in this country brings to mind the airplane pilot who announced over the loudspeaker to the passengers that he had "good news and bad news. First the good news: we have a very strong tail wind and have an almost unprecedented ground speed of 700 miles an hour. Now for the bad news; our instrument panel isn't working, so we don't know where we're going—but we're sure getting there fast!"

Obscenity wasn't regarded as an offense in this country until the 1880's, when Massachusetts became the first state to adopt a law against it. The anti-obscenity forces flowered in the Victorian era and were epitomized in the federal Comstock Act (see Chapter I). That act prohibited the importation, or carriage by mail or in interstate commerce, of "every obscene, lewd, lascivious, indecent, filthy, or vile article, matter, thing, device, or substance." Many states adopted identical or similar "little Comstock Acts," and a number of cities and towns followed suit. But despite the anti-obscenity laws, the courts ruled that the test of obscenity was its "probable effect on not the most susceptible person in the community, but the average person."

All this was fine until the Supreme Court handed down a recent decision that a material could be banned as pornographic if it was "patently offensive," appealed to the "prurient" interest, and lacked serious literary, artistic, political, or scientific value. Further, the Supreme Court held, a judge or a jury could apply standards of their own "community" in making such determinations, rather than trying to apply some sort of national standard.

What Do the Critics Think?

Clive Barnes, drama critic of the New York *Times* says: "Censorship is a dirty word—perhaps the dirtiest. The easiest thing to censor—or if you prefer it, to suppress—is something of a sexual nature. You merely have to say that it offends you morally, and in breathless, bible-tapping guilt, a considerable part of the community is likely to support you."

Dr. Alex Comfort, editor of *The Joy of Sex*, adds: "Normal people enjoy looking at sex books and reading sex fantasies; that's why abnormal people spend so much time and money suppressing them ... normal people use pornography as football enthusiasts use books about football—as a real help in raising the level of feeling to bed level."

Dr. H.J. Campbell, author of *The Pleasure Areas*, says: "Perhaps the inability of reformers to demonstrate a connection between pornography and sexual behavior is because these are, in fact, poorly related. Pornography may be viewed as simply self-stimulation by the visual channel, having no deeper or longer-lasting effect than the visual pleasure of looking at a sunset. If pornography were increasing while other sensory pleasures were not, there might be cause for alarm. At present the alarming situation is that so many forms of sensory pleasure are mounting rapidly."

Supreme Court Justice William O. Douglas commented recently: "... should a publication whose main impact is the arousal of sexual desires be banned? A goodly part of life is the arousal of sexual desires ...

"The real purpose of censorship is to make the public live up to the censor's code of morality. The vice of the test that makes arousal of sexual appetites a basis for condemning a book, an article, or a movie is that it enables one censor, who is a prude, to ban Shakespeare or even "The Song of Solomon" while it enables another to follow blindly the list of banned books which some group has at hand.

"Sex cannot be suppressed in life. Should it be attempted in literature ... ?"

Even a noted religious leader who is generally against all erotic art said: "Talk about censorship? I call this obscene. This is an obscenity to me that is far worse than anything sexual might be."

Critic Barnes adds: " ... in art there is an enormous difference, in intention if nothing else measurable, between the erotic and the pornographic.

"Eroticism is to the artist the expression of a very precious part of life. The artist's intention is not pornography but truth. Eroticism is woven into the web of his words and offered as part of life ...

"Artists should not be censored—but neither should they imagine that their own standards of taste are universal ... Our arts must be free, but they also must be careful ... "

Perhaps one of the most realistic criticisms of pornography came from a patron, who said: "The trouble with pornographic films is that there is no such thing as a sex problem in them. The guy and the girl meet; they undress each other, and each one knows exactly what the other likes. It's a perfect match every time though they're never supposed to have seen each other before. That's carrying fantasy too far.

"What I'd like to see is an old-fashioned love story showing how a couple who care about each other learn gradually how to bring each other to the heights. I'd like to see how it looks explicitly when the guy or gal is pushing the wrong buttons . . . "

This concept is supported by Dr. Avodah Offit, head of the Lenox Hill Hospital's Sexual Therapy and Consultation Center, New York, who says:

"My own feeling is that pornography is related to sex and sex is related to love, but pornography is not necessarily related to love or to what our society considers the most fulfilled kind of sexual relationship. I would like to see much more explicit material available to show what a good relationship can be like sexually, as well as material that might depict the awkwardness and difficulties of sexual frustration and failure. I'd like people to be able, through the media, to experience sex as it really is.

"Ideal sexuality, like the ideal housewife, is a myth that ought to be more openly dispelled . . . "

Like it or not, pornography will be with us . . . although it may have a long way to go before its "social value" outweighs its sexual value. Meanwhile, you can pay your money and take your choice. Pornography may not be for everybody, but not everybody has to be for pornography. Perhaps the most important problem with pornography is to prevent it from coming upon one unexpectedly.

Most doctors agree that if an explicit film degrades or demeans one sex or the other (or both sexes), then the experience isn't beneficial. But if the couples who see the movie gain new ideas or freedom, then the film serves come purpose.

It should be available—and clearly marked—for people who want it. But pornography should not arrive unannounced through the mails, nor should it be casually displayed or sold within reach of those who might innocently stumble on it and are not prepared for it. There's probably nothing worse than sexual exploitation of a person who is not psychologically prepared for it. In this case, matter gets the better of the mind.

XI
IS SEXUAL VARIETY
THE SPICE OF LIFE?

Findings based upon controlled samples of homosexuals and heterosexuals lead many authorities to agree that homosexuality may be within a normal psychological range, and that it is more a sexual "variation" than "deviation."

Figures compiled at the Institute for Sex Research indicate that between adolescence and old age about 37 percent of all males have some overt homosexual experience to the point of orgasm; that over half of the males who remain unmarried at age thirty-five have homosexual experience; and that about 4 percent of all white males are exclusively homosexual all their lives. Estimated female homosexuality (lesbianism) is about half that of males.

Whereas American society worships youth, the homosexual community places even greater emphasis on this fleeting characteristic. The homosexual has fewer outlets and opportunities, and he has no wife or children to "cushion" his old age. About half of homosexuals' contacts may be with persons they have sex with only once. Between 10 and 20 percent of homosexual contacts are made at public terminals and other public and semipublic locations. Many homosexual affairs last less than one year. About one-quarter of homosexuals report that kissing occurred in one-third or less of their sexual contacts.

Given the transitory nature of homosexual contacts, age may place an increasing burden on the homosexual, who must be attractive enough to snare fleeting "romances." Other studies have shown, however, that once over the hurdle of aging, older homosexuals tend to be better adjusted socially and psychologically than younger ones.

Other studies explode some myths about homosexuals: they don't prey on young children or wish they were heterosexual; they aren't more creative or artistic than heterosexuals (lumbermen, miners, and cattlemen practice homosexuality as well as artists); and they *don't* have distinguishing physical characteristics (although some may show some mannerisms).

It should also be mentioned that the overwhelming majority of homosexuals are not transvestites (in fact, many transvestites are determinedly heterosexual), nor do they have transsexual desires. Most "gays" are outwardly indistinguishable from the rest of the population. Most lesbians are not "butch," and most male homosexuals are not particularly effeminate. Virile, masculine-appearing businessmen frequent many so-called gay entertainment spots, and yet they may perform heterosexually at home. Many famous personalities of history—Michelangelo, André Gide, Marcel Proust, W. Somerset Maugham, E.M. Forster, among others—were overt or latent homosexuals.

How Do Homosexuals Get That Way?

Recently some graffiti was observed on a wall: "My mother made me a homosexual." Next to it was scrawled: "If I get her the wool, will she make me one too?"

It may not be a very good joke, but psychiatrists who treat homosexuals consistently point to disturbed relations between the parent and child, although there may be little childhood seduction by an adult of the same sex.

Freudian psychologists maintain that homosexuality may develop along two paths: (1) in the absence of a father, or in the presence of a weak or alcoholic one, the boy-child falls in love with his mother; but he panics at the thought of incest and suppresses sexual feelings toward women in general; or (2) in an opposite manner, the child falls in love with the parent of the same sex and attempts to oust the parent of the opposite sex.

Other causes may include fear of sex consequences (pregnancy or venereal disease), fear of inadequacy, or inability to play the male or female role. In practice it is not unusual to find a combination of these factors, in greater or lesser degree.

Lesbianism may also be associated with a poor parental relationship, especially with the father. Few lesbians wish to pattern themselves after either parent, especially the father, who may have been weak or frightening.

Other causes of lesbianism may include: (1) strong love for the father and identification with a male figure; (2) jealousy of the male's favored role in society; and (3) sexual maleducation that teaches that men are dirty and untouchable and that women are "pure."

In general, lesbians form more durable relations than male homosexuals. They seldom "cruise" looking for pickups, and they are less concerned with genital stimulation than are men. Ironically, the lesbian usually acts in accordance with biological and cultural factors that make her a woman, and the male homosexual acts in accordance with the factors that make him a man.

The lesbian "stereotype" is as distorted as the stereotype of the male homosexual. The unattractive, clumsy "butch" can become a homosexual as well as the beautiful girl who is enamored of her own beauty and seeks a reflection of it in another female.

Why are there fewer lesbians than male homosexuals? Sociologists believe that a female's lower sex drive, the wider opportunities for outlets, and the fact that more women than men can lead basically "sexless" lives all contribute to the lower incidence of lesbianism. Also, lesbians often lead more discreet lives than male homosexuals and often find it possible to accept, with some degree of frigidity, sexual relations with a husband.

Society tends to see male homosexuality as a barrier to reproduction and wasteful of semen, whereas lesbianism isn't socially "harmful." People also tend to be condescending toward lesbians because they view them as unfortunate women who aren't able to attract a mate. And in a male-dominated society in which men acquire all kinds of goods, two women making love don't threaten a man as two homosexuals might.

Do We All Have Homosexual Capacities?

Dr. Wardell Pomeroy, coauthor of the Kinsey reports, says that we aren't born homosexual or heterosexual, but we're born with the capacity to respond sexually. How we respond depends to a large extent on what experiences we have as we mature.

Experiences in a heterosexual culture usually lead us to develop that way, but even in the same set of circumstances, one person becomes a homosexual and another heterosexual.

At the Kinsey Institute, researchers devised a scale, from zero to six, to rate degrees of homosexuality and heterosexuality; zero is completely heterosexual; six is completely homosexual. Scientists say that most people fall somewhere in between these extremes; thus everyone is at least capable—given certain circumstances—of relating or responding homosexually.

Using this scale, Kinsey found that 4 percent of white males are exclusively homosexual throughout their lives after the onset of adolescence; 8 percent are exclusively homosexual for at least three years between the ages of sixteen and fifty-five; 10 percent are more or less exclusively homosexual for such a three-year period; and 13 percent are more homosexual than heterosexual for this three-year period.

As to females, between 2 and 6 percent of unmarried females and less than 1 percent of married females in the Kinsey sample are more or less exclusively homosexual between the ages of twenty and thirty-five.

Male and female homosexuals don't particularly like one another, but they sometimes join the same groups, such as the Mattachine Society, which includes members of both sexes.

Do Homosexuals Want to Be "Cured?"

Dr. Lawrence LeShan, a member of the Association for Humanistic Psychology, agrees with most psychologists when he says that the extent to which a disturbed homosexual might be "cured" depends more upon the patient's motivation than upon the clinical treatment.

Just recently the American Psychiatric Association has altered a position it had held for almost a century. Its new official position states that homosexuality should no longer be considered a mental disease but a "sexual orientation disturbance." This means that a homosexual who was at peace with himself would not be considered in need of psychotherapy and that only a homosexual who was distressed about his sexual orientation would be thought of as disturbed and to require help. The A.P.A. also issued a statement urging the repeal of all legislation (currently existing in about forty states) that makes criminal offenses of sexual acts performed by consenting adults in private.

Currently, most clinicians try to help homosexuals to accept their homosexuality and to express it in personally and societally rewarding ways. Dr. LeShan says: "Curing the homosexuality has never been my goal. What I am interested in is how the individual feels about himself as a person . . . Both homosexuals and heterosexuals can lead lives of quiet despair and self-destruction, or they can in their love relationships, in whatever forms these may take, express a profound sense of self and a capacity to give lovingly to another person."

Other clinicians say they aim to relieve the hostility toward and fear of relationships, sexual and other, with the other sex. They do this for two reasons: (1) to help the homosexual get at the root of the problem and not to attack what is merely a symptom; and (2) to assure the homosexual that his present pleasures and gratifications won't be removed, but will be enhanced without guilt feelings.

Given the above conditions, a successful therapeutic program would leave the male patient interested in actively seeking gratification with females as well as being attracted to males—relieved of fear and anxiety in both relationships.

In spite of these advances on the psychiatric front, some doctors consider "aversion therapy" the proper treatment for homosexuality. Aversion therapy uses electric shock, drugs, and mental suggestion to make an act distasteful. In one common treatment, a male homosexual is wired to a device that measures involuntary sexual response, and he is then shown slides of nude men alternating with slides of nude women. When he responds to a male slide he receives a shock until he presses a button, which brings on the female slide and relief from the shock.

Aversion therapy often is used with homosexuals as a last resort, and many psychiatrists oppose it. Charles Silverstein, director of the Institute for Human Identity, a New York counseling center for homosexuals, calls the treatment "a technique of violence in the name of science."

Sometimes aversion therapy works too well. Dr. Newton Dieter, a Los Angeles clinical psychologist, says he is treating a former practicing homosexual who was aversively conditioned, "cured," and later married. Dr. Dieter adds: "But now he is incapable of forming male friendships. If he shakes a man's hand, he becomes physically ill."

Aversion therapy, also, does not guarantee that the patient will become attracted to the opposite sex once he has been made adverse to members of his own sex. In fact, a number of patients who have undergone aversion therapy have become practically asexual. Furthermore, the effects of this type of therapy have not proven to be permanent in many cases.

Is a "New" Homosexuality" Emerging?

Some psychiatrists believe that a "new" form of homosexuality may be emerging that is more "bisexual" in nature. A woman who runs a "gay" bar said: "When my bar first opened, a woman was either a 'butch' and as such assumed the male role of dominance and aggressiveness, or she was a 'femme' and assumed the female role of passivity and submission. The 'new lesbian' doesn't see the world through gay-colored glasses. She can have relations with both sexes without having to classify them as 'straight' or 'gay.' "

Many women also feel that true bisexuality is the best alternative for the really liberated woman. Far from being a threat to men, the new lesbian will make things easier. She is less likely to be passive, since she is more aware of herself sexually, and she is less likely to treat men as sexual objects since she knows the complications and game-playing involved.

Women's Liberation has helped to "bring out" many women. One woman said: "Women's Lib has changed the deep patterns of competition for men. We've begun to be open, honest, and able to cooperate. During these changes I've felt a new commitment to women. I also am able to accept men as friends and lovers again. Perhaps the Movement has been responsible for my and other women's greater mellowness and openness to men."

Many social scientists have observed that, given a society free from sex-role definition, every man and woman would be bisexual. Since this situation doesn't exist now, the new lesbian is a force for change.

Men also may become more bisexual. One woman in her late forties told how she accidentally found among her husband's belongings a book listing "gay" restaurants and cocktail lounges all over the country, pamphlets with male nudes in all kinds of positions, vaseline, and even a vibrator.

The woman was reluctant to confront her husband with this evidence because their own sexual relations were good and she didn't want to destroy them. But she went to a counselor, who said: "If your marriage remains as successful as you describe, I see no reason why anything should have to change between you .... It may well be that his apparent homosexuality is quite secondary to his love for you."

Recent findings suggest that sexual identity is neither fixed at an early age nor stable throughout a lifetime. Dr. Pepper Schwartz, a sociologist who is studying bisexuality at the University of Washington, says: " . . . what you are at twenty-one is not necessarily the same as what you are at forty-one."

Bisexuality in "Threesomes" and Groups
In threesomes and groups, which are becoming more "socially

acceptable" (see Chapter XII), bisexual opportunities are inevitable.

Usually, however, only the women perform bisexually; this activity "turns on" men. Although some women may worry that this makes them "gay," there's little evidence that it does.

One married man told how he persuaded his wife to enter into a threesome to the benefit of all: "There's a difference between a man doing what he thinks pleases a woman, even when she gives him suggestions, and another woman doing it. You have to see it to get the ideas. Now that I've watched, I've become a better lover."

Dr. Alex Comfort, editor of *The Joy of Sex*, says: "Males in most cultures do, or would, play sex games together under some circumstances . . . apes certainly do. If we didn't have this capacity, humans might never have formed male societies, because erotic play between same-sex partners helps to override the rivalry and fighting we see in some other societies."

Many doctors feel that homosexuals and heterosexuals have more in common than they do differences, and that any homosexual "traits" result more from a hostile environment than from personality traits. Just as heterosexuals need warmth and love, so do homosexuals, although they may not have as many opportunities. As Dr. Wardell Pomeroy said: "I have seen many homosexuals who were happy, who were participating and conscientious members of their community, and who were stable, productive, warm, relaxed, and efficient."

Are Older People More Often Sex Offenders?

Some segments of society tend to picture both the child molester and the exhibitionist as "dirty old men." But this is a part of the stereotyped thinking that denies sexuality in the aging or considers it as some form of aberration.

Donald Mulcock, child welfare specialist, in studying men who assaulted children sexually in England and Wales, found that most offenses against boys were committed by men between the ages of thirty-nine and fifty, and those against girls by men between ages thirty-three and forty-four. Only 6 percent of the men he studied were sixty-three, and none were older.

Unhappily, the older man who shows affection to a child not his own is still suspect by society and may even face a prison term for an innocent gesture.

Frederick E. Whiskin, assistant in psychiatry at the Harvard Medical School, believes that a great deal of the sexual behavior of elderly men is not basically genital in origin, but flows from their emotional isolation and yearning for the warmth and comfort of contact with youth. When an older woman hugs and fondles children it is considered natural; when an older man does this, he's often considered a "dirty old man."

Certain aberrations, however, may persist into extreme old age. One woman tells of a great-uncle, who, when he was in his nineties and she was in puberty, was always trying to lift her skirts to take some "feels." When he was ninety-seven he had a housekeeper who stayed only a little while, complaining: "That old man tries to lift my dress, pinches me, feels my breasts, and suggests we go to bed." A second housekeeper left for the same reasons. A third one stayed on, leading the grandniece to speculate either that she complied, was too unattractive, or the old man finally cooled off.

Should Sexual Variations Be Classed as Crimes?

Kinsey once remarked that if the sex laws were strictly enforced in the United States, about 99 percent of the men would be in jail. Almost every state has laws like California which states: "Any person participating in an act of copulating the mouth of one person with the sexual organ of another is punishable by imprisonment in the state prison for not exceeding 15 years .... The order of commitment shall expressly state whether a person convicted hereunder is more than 10 years older than his coparticipant and whether such coparticipant is under the age of 14 ... "

Unfortunately, this law—and probably many others—does not distinguish between relationships; oral copulation between husband and wife is just as much a crime as that between a man and a woman not his wife, a man and man, or a man and a minor.

Many statutes listing sex offenses are vaguely worded and include such terms as "carnal abuse," "open lewdness," "sodomy," and "unnatural practices" that can mean almost anything and vary widely in meaning from one legislative jurisdiction to another.

Sex offenders aren't necessarily sex deviates or perverts, and they may not be psychologically disturbed. Statutory rape is considered common in most parts of the world and is usually considered psychologically normal.

Dr. Albert Ellis, the well known psychotherapist, says that it is not true that anyone who enjoys oral-genital, anal-genital, and other extracoital acts as well as regular intercourse is perverted. In fact, he says: "From a psychological standpoint, it may justifiably be said that some individuals who *only* engage in penile-vaginal intercourse and under no circumstances even try noncoital methods of heterosexual relations are extremely fetishistic and fearful and hence, tend, in a minor sort of way, to be deviated."

Thus, many charges of sex deviations might be made against the "good" person who feels there is only one way—his/her way—of having "lawful" sex.

Lawyers say that in some cases "mean, hard wives" make charges of sex crimes against their husbands (when both partners have participated in the act) to obtain a "cheap" divorce. In some states, if a husband is charged with a felony and imprisoned, the wife can automatically obtain a divorce because of the felony conviction—at no expense to her.

Kinsey, Masters and Johnson, and other sexologists say that "unlawful" sex practices are the norm rather than the exception in most marriages, and that no one should be punished for them.

Sex laws also fail to take into account the possibility of awakened sensuality in later years. Bernard Berenson, who died at the age of ninety-four, wrote, "I only really became aware of sex and of women's physical, animal life at the period that might be called my old age."

In his middle years, Auguste Rodin had little time for women, but when he reached age seventy, he became extremely attentive to them. He said: "I did not know that I could scorn women at twenty and be charmed by them at seventy."

Leon Trotsky felt he was old at age fifty-five, but at fifty-eight he had an odd outburst of eroticism not only for his wife, but also for a younger partner.

History and literature are filled with older people who found new sexual delights at advanced years. Should they (or anyone) be denied them if both partners are willing and no one gets hurt? Although we've come far in sexual freedom, we're still bound by old, restrictive laws.

Besides the physical and emotional aspects sex has legal aspects that may become complicated in a late or second marriage, or in any "arrangement" that may not have the blessings of either the clergy or the Internal Revenue Service. In the next chapter we shall examine some legal sides to later marriage as well as some "extralegal" relationships in which older couples may find more satisfying lifestyles.

XII
THE BEST IS YET TO COME?

Does the way we live affect the way we love? Or does the way we love affect the way we live? Whatever your answer, the person you live with, how and where you live all influence your love life. In turn, your love life affects whom you live with, where, how . . .

Today you may choose among many more acceptable life and love styles. These include traditional marriage; singles society; group arrangements; communes; retirement communities; young-old relationships; future sex; and just plain love—all in flexible combinations.

If you choose wisely, your September song will be sweet for yourself and your love. Let's examine the possibilities to see how we can enhance present life-styles and explore other arrangements for better living and loving.

"Till Death Do Us Part? . . . "

William Lederer and the late Dr. Donald Jackson, authors of *The Mirages of Marriage*, say that the partners of many marriages fail to recognize certain *realities.* By not doing so, they expect too much. Here are some basic realities:

1. *People don't marry because they "fall madly in love."* Psychiatrist Harry Stack Sullivan says: "When the satisfaction or the security of another person becomes as significant to one as one's own satisfaction or security, then the state of love exists." By this definition, what most people take for love is something else: a strong sex drive, a fear of being unloved, a hunger for approval.

2. *Love is NOT necessary for a satisfactory marriage.* You achieve a working marriage if both parties feel they are better off together than separate. They may not be "in love," but they aren't lonely and they share contentment.

173

3. *You can disagree with your spouse and still have a good marriage.* People are different, with different interests, attitudes, biological rhythms. Conflicts arise; there must be compromises. But one person *can't* constantly give in to another or do something distasteful.

If we accept these realities and resolve our conflicts about them, we may have a smooth marriage. As we grow older, rough edges should be worn smoother. However, the same old routine, repeated too often, loses its punch, and we get bored. A sixty-three-year-old man complained that his lovemaking was in a rut: "My wife feels it's all right to let the sex drive die down and will do nothing to keep it alive. At my age I need more stimulation, and hence more participation from my wife. Am I unusual in desiring more participation from her?"

Numerous women complain that their own sexual interests are more intense than their husbands', and that the "old boy needs pepping up" to keep the marriage alive and exciting.

Whatever the cause, men are more subject to a "psychic saturation point." From middle age onward the wife must jolt her husband out of his rut and introduce adventure and romance into their lives. This becomes all the more important as the man approaches retirement.

Retirement: Danger Time for Marriage?

On a "stress impact chart" designed by Dr. Thomas H. Holmes, professor of psychiatry at the University of Washington, death of a spouse leads the impact list with a relative stress value of 100. Marriage ranks seventh with a value of 50; retirement tenth with a value of 45. Divorce, children leaving home, marriage cause a bit more stress.

However it happens, if you acquire more than 300 stress points in a year, you've reached the danger point. In the population sample Dr. Holmes studied, 80 percent who exceeded 300 stress points became seriously depressed, had heart attacks, or suffered serious illness. Even those who exceeded 200 stress points suffered a disruptive illness. These stressful events may happen when we're more set in our ways and have fewer options. We may prefer familar people, places, and things . . . old ways of doing things, and a certain comfortable life-style.

Too much change in too short a time carries a psychological price tag . . . the more radical the changes, or the greater the number, the steeper the price.

Unfortunately approaching retirement—and retirement itself—puts a special strain on marriage. Persons who could live together in the evenings and on weekends face the possibility that it might be harder to communicate with and tolerate each other during a long retirement day.

Experts say the five danger signs for a retirement marriage are: financial problems, immaturity, lack of communication, boredom, and the "empty nest syndrome."

A man may seek to compensate for his diminishing role as the breadwinner, and his retirement uncertainties and frustration, by demanding excessive service and attention. A wife may respond by nagging. After retirement, the man who was wrapped up in his job and the wife who was wrapped up in her children may find that they have fewer interests in common.

To avoid marital stresses before and after retirement, counselors make the following suggestions:

• Plan your finances for now and in retirement. A good marriage should be a good business partnership; money planning "cushions" stress.

• Plan togetherness and separate activities to fill the hours. Assure privacy with a den, a sewing room, a study; respect each other's routines, friends, and conversations.

• Develop some common interests. A joint hobby, business, community-service project, political campaign can help stimulate each other's activities and involvement and assure something to talk about and to plan for.

• Keep open the lines of communication. Now and in retirement you'll need to talk with each other more than ever.

You need to plan not only for today—but for the tomorrow when your husband or wife may become alone.

The Need to Talk—to Yourself and to Your Spouse

Lack of communication leads to misunderstandings. Dr. David Kahn, a clinical psychologist at the Merrill-Palmer Institute, presented couples with a sentence-completion test made up of statements such as: "Personal habits of mine which annoy my mate most are ... " "Things would go better if he (she) would tell me ... " The husband and wife each filled out two forms, one in which they answered as they *thought* their mates would answer, and another in which they completed the statements for themselves.

Comparison of answers showed that mates didn't understand or even know each other very well. In their book *Open Marriage,* Nena and George O'Neill write: "Unless you tell your mate how you feel, he or she will be forced to guess, and the strong likelihood is that the guess will be wrong. Communication can't be carried out on the basis of supposition; mind-reading is best left in the hands of nightclub performers."

They suggest that you try to be honest with yourself. Take time off to be alone, and use that time to carry on an active inner dialogue, using revelation, self-analysis, and reevaluation. You may come up with an unflattering analysis of your behavior, but you'll discover ways to communicate better with yourself—to understand why you acted as you did—and perhaps to prevent miscommunication with your mate.

The O'Neills also suggest that if there's something you can't yet tell your mate—because you're too shy or angry or because your mate gets angry when you bring up the subject—try recording what you want to say on tape (or write it out), then let your mate play it back (or read it) in private. You can also test your own reaction to the message, as you'll be able to hear it or read it as though you were a third person, removed from your emotional involvement in the immediate situation.

Remember, too, that a little extrasexual communcation—discussion of problems, books, records, music, movies—improves sexual activity and enjoyment.

The O'Neills also say that it's important for you to learn of "hook-up points" (your likes, dislikes, sex preferences, etc.). No matter how many hook-up points you share, however, you can't share them all. Unfortunately, these contact points are part of you, and if not used or touched, they'll become brittle and may die. This destroys your uniqueness. If a hook-up point is deeply imbedded in your personality, you can't shed it like a porcupine's quill. Dr. Abraham Maslow says: "Capacities clamor to be used, and cease their clamor only when they are well used . . . . Not only is it fun to use our capacities, but it is also necessary for growth. The unused skill or capacity or organ can become a disease center or else atrophy or disappear, thus diminishing the person."

As far as hook-up points involving sex, most psychologists say that *you shouldn't force yourself* to do anything that you don't really want to do. Better that your mate seek the satisfaction elsewhere than seek it with a reluctant you.

What Alternatives to Traditional Marriage?

"You can't really expect a person to eat the same meal for dinner every day for the rest of his life and not get tired of it. I don't expect my husband to make love only to me for the rest of his life. Few men are ever that faithful," says one emancipated woman.

A French psychiatrist adds: "Americans are simply *ridiculous!* Human beings are *not* monogamous creatures—and with the increasing longevity and general good health until people are quite old, it is insane to expect them to be faithful to one love relationship. Since it is an impossible goal, it almost never works out that way."

Affairs have always been part of the male-oriented world. The Kinsey studies showed that by age forty, half of all husbands and a quarter of the wives had outside affairs. Interestingly, the Kinsey studies may have contributed to affairs. Said one woman: "Kinsey probably screwed up a whole generation by saying that the average couple of a certain age were having sex a certain number of times a week—when maybe only once a week was good enough for them. They might feel guilty about not getting enough, so they go out to prove themselves."

Increasingly, people feel less guilty about having affairs. Said one young woman having a liaison with a middle-aged husband: "The fact that he is married means nothing. In the deepest sense we clicked together because we can communicate ... I don't feel guilty at all. His married life is something different, and I can't claim to affect that. I see our relationship as something between him and me, and I'm not out to gain possession."

Men aren't the only ones having affairs. The Women's Liberation movement, and more liberal sexual and moral attitudes, have convinced many women that they have a right to sexual fulfillment if they don't get it at home.

A woman may even have a successful husband, nonneurotic children, and a comfortable home with comfortable trimmings. But the husband may be wrapped up in his career, and the wife might be socially climbing. If she sacrifices marital lovemaking for financial security, she might take a lover.

A forty-five-year-old woman, married to a prominent lawyer, says she averages one-and-a-half lovers per year. She adds. "I have a wonderful marriage, but sex with my husband is miserable. Once a month isn't enough for me, so I'm always having affairs with some one. It's the most reasonable solution; look at my alternatives—celibacy or divorce."

Can Mate-Swapping Save a Marriage?

One couple (he's forty-seven; she's forty-four) say they "saved" their marriage through mate-swapping. The husband, Frank, said he "swung" before his marriage, and his second wife, Peg, enjoyed varied sex before she married Frank.

They usually mate-swap with couples Frank knew in the old days, but sometimes they answer ads in "swinger" newspapers available in major cities. If they establish rapport through a telephone call, they arrange to meet the other couple in a cocktail bar.

During a couple of drinks they size up the other couple. They've worked out a set of signals to let each other know how they feel about the possibilities. If they both signal willingness, they invite the other couple back to the apartment.

When Frank and Peg were interviewed by a team of psychologists, Peg remarked: "It's hard to evaluate mate-swapping's effect on our marriage because it's been part of our relationship from the beginning. But I feel that part of the reason we're comfortable is that we're not frustrating each other or standing in each other's way."

Dr. Ruth Shonle Cavan, adjunct professor of sociology, Northern Illinois University, says: "Comarital relationships or mate-swapping or swinging also seems adaptable to the old. Some intimate relationships become stale with time but give enough satisfaction that the couple does not wish to dissolve them. Comarital relationships tend to be practiced in small groups or clubs ... the club is protective of marriage: it meets privately, conceals its activities from children, neighbors, and the police, and frowns upon any tendency of members to consistently pair off with the same person and thus threaten the marriage. At present it is an activity of middle-class, middle-aged adults. It seems to have possibilities for older people who wish to add variety and sparkle to their marriage."

Opposition to mate-swapping comes from a surprising source: Dr. Robert Chartham, who says in *Your Sexual Future*: "I am opposed to mate-swapping, not because I am square, but because I have evidence that there are dangers to the marriage relationship inherent in it." He feels that the fact that mate-swapping condones adultery means that the relationship has lost meaning.

If Two's a Company, Three's a . . . ?

The ancient Greeks, Romans, and Indians believed it . . . Shelley and Casanova practiced it. It's called "troilism"—when a couple and a third person make love to one another at the same time. Usually, the threesome consists of two women and a man. The pattern includes joint foreplay followed by the man's engaging in oral sex with both women or making love orally to one while having coitus with the other. Usually, the women engage in mutual cunnilingus; they not only desire it, but it's a "turn on" for the man. The women seldom fear lesbian relationships. Says one woman: "I can have sex with a woman without fearing that I'm a lesbian because there's a man there to assure me that I'm normal."

Dr. George Weinberg, author of *Society and the Healthy Homo-sexual*, believes that troilism offers spice and variety to a conventional marriage because the experience offers a couple the stimulation of seeing the person they care for in the eyes of a third party. And while a spouse may concentrate for moments on the third party, the emphasis is on the couple.

Gay Talese, author of books on the American sexual revolution, says that while youngsters are more natural about threesomes, it's the middle-aged ones that see it as something odd. However, studies have shown that some middle-aged couples would like to try a threesome if no one knew about it.

While most threesomes are casual or short-term relationships, one couple, both in their forties and married twenty-two years, invited a forty-five-year-old widow to move in with them and even to change her name to theirs. They spend holidays as a trio, and if anyone questions the relationship, they claim the two women are sisters.

One woman sounds a negative note to threesomes. She tells about being picked up by a couple during intermission at a theater and being invited to spend the weekend. The visit developed into a threesome, but the woman found that the wife was using "swinging" to humiliate her husband, constantly making nasty remarks about what a poor lover he was.

Some countries have even legalized threesomes. The West German Bundesrat gave its approval to legislation legalizing group sex, wife-swapping, and the sale of pornographic materials.

After Divorce—What?

At present about one in every three marriages ends in divorce. Today about 25 percent of divorces are among couples married fifteen years and longer, and since 1963 divorce among couples married for twenty to twenty-four years has increased by 28 percent.

Sociologist Margaret Mead blames the high divorce rate on our changing notions of marriage. She says: "We no longer believe that two people who get married should try to weather storms that shake any vital, intimate relationship."

Perhaps the media give us such a glossy image of middle-class happiness that we expect too much. Says Dr. Richard E. Farson of the Esalen Institute: "The implication that a constant state of affection and unity in family life is actually achievable gives rise to dissatisfactions in one's own marriage. The media's message is regarded as a major source of the 'cultural tone' in which people are more aware of their emotional needs."

The changing legal picture makes divorces easier to get and more frequent. Among the changes are do-it-yourself divorce, no-fault divorce, alimony to either party, and property settlements less contingent on who breaks up the marriage.

Sex still causes most divorces. People expect that marriage will provide companionship, intimacy, love, "peak experience" of all kinds. When they don't happen, people feel cheated. In *The Wonderful Crisis of Middle Age,* Eda LeShan says: "For the middle-aged woman the current preoccupation with sexual technique rather than feeling and relationships is especially unsettling. A charming lady of 63 told me: 'I read *The Sensuous Woman* and I knew I was a complete bust as a woman. Never mind that my husband and I have been married 35 years and love each other more than ever. We are obviously failures, because I'd rather *die* than do most of the things in that book!'"

Perhaps more sensitive reality might produce more sensible expectations. Happiness means attainable goals, not the goals in the media or in most sex manuals.

Because of, or in spite of, sexual dissatisfactions, divorced persons salvage wounded egos with sensuous sex. A study by P. Gebhart in *Divorce and After* shows that three-fourths of young divorced woman had nonmarital coitus; at age fifty-six to sixty, 43 percent were having affairs.

After divorce a person's sexual self-esteem sinks to a new low. A smorgasbord approach to new sexual experience satisfies the ego and avoids emotional entanglements. Most divorced persons (especially women) suspect they've missed something and rush to make it up. One forty-five-year-old woman says she has reorganized her sexual habits from top to bottom . . . picked up men fifteen years her junior, dabbled with group sex, mastered oral and anal sex. "Why not?" she says. "For years I was little Miss Priss, the faithful dogsbody who never played around, never complained when he didn't satisfy me. Now, don't I owe myself a treat?"

Most divorcées also suffer from the "teddy bear syndrome"— the desire to have a warm body to cuddle at night. Unaccustomed to sleeping alone, the divorcée tries to fill the vacancy one way or another. But some women would rather sit at home and . . . as one woman said: "Every man thinks a divorcée is ripe for sex. If you don't give in on the first date, they never call again. Even if you do, there's still a chance they'll never call again. So until somebody human comes along, I'll sit home and masturbate."

Even crusaders for casual relations find the sex search begins to pall. One active divorcée said: "At first, sleeping around was great, but after several months I felt like I had gorged on chocolate cake, and I suddenly craved a meat-and-potatoes relationship."

But here's the danger. One thrice-wed matron advises: "The worst thing about ending a marriage is that in the back of your mind you know damned well that you're just going to find another worthless bastard and do it all over again." Statistics show that about 90 percent of divorcées or widows remarry, and about 60 percent find new mates within eighteen months of losing their old ones. However, about 80 percent of those who don't remarry are women, and the women may take twice as long as men to find new partners.

Maybe more divorced women don't remarry because they can find new freedom and opportunities in organizations like the National Organization for Women (NOW), which recently spotlighted the divorced woman, calling for divorce insurance for women. Said Betty Friedan, one of the founders of NOW: "If divorce has increased by 1,000 percent don't blame the women's movement. Blame the obsolete sex roles on which our marriages are based."

Other divorcées (also widows, widowers, and separated men) in their forties and fifties are finding new outlets in organizations like Parents Without Partners, an international nonprofit, nonsectarian educational organization devoted to the welfare and interests of single parents and their children. One forty-nine-year-old widower with seven children says that through P.W.P. he has dated and sometimes taken joint picnics with his brood and the families of widows he has met at club meetings. "Parents Without Partners is a good deal," he says. "They're respectable people." The organization has chapters in many cities; for the address of the chapter nearest you, you can write P.W.P., 7910 Woodmont Avenue, Washington, D.C. 20014.

Psychologists say it takes a divorced person about a year to get over depression and dislocation. They advise that if you move into a club or hotel you should plan to stay only a short time. They also warn against any serious emotional entanglements until you are well over your divorce. One psychiatrist recommends avoiding another marriage for at least a year or two.

Dr. Walter C. McKain, of the University of Connecticut, says the five characteristics to look for in a mate in a late or second marriage are enthusiasm, ability to accept responsibility, a feeling that the person's life is useful and important, pride in appearance, and a cheerful, optimistic mood. Gerontologist Dr. Lorraine H. Clark adds: "If a man doesn't speak well of his first wife, he probably won't speak well of his second." She says this applies to women as well as men.

And Dr. McKain concludes: "Couples who have known each other a long time or had mutual friends had better marriages than couples who were self-introduced. If they were entertained by their children before the marriage, they were more likely to succeed because they had their families' approval and support."

Don't overlook the legal aspects of a late or second marriage. In some instances, divorce cuts off future social security benefits to a wife or reduces the amount. Also, some states have laws that partially or completely invalidate your old will when you remarry; any transfer or change of title of a house or wealth may incur tax liabilities or lead to unhappiness.

In many cases you can sign a prenuptial agreement—a written contract between you and your prospective spouse signed before marriage and in contemplation of marriage—that specifies who owns what. Such an agreement is sometimes necessary if you want to will property to children by a first marriage.

The Singles Society: Divorcées, Widows, Unmarrieds

The force, number, and visibility of middle-aged divorcées establish the older "singles society," and the 10 million widows (vs. 2 million widowers) expand it. Whether widowed, divorced, or unmarried, "singles" can move into a singles apartment, go to a singles bar, or take a singles trip and find dozens of companions.

Singles are free to experiment sexually, although some widows feel that social disapproval dampens sexual activity (only 25 percent of widows age fifty-six to sixty report sexual activity). Psychiatrist Karl M. Bowman believes, however, that many widows don't have sexual relations because they are afraid they have lost their power to please, and they don't want their pride hurt. They may feel lonely, isolated, deprived, unwanted, insecure. "To prevent these feelings," says Dr. Bowman, "they need to have as active a sex life as possible and to enjoy it without fear."

Probably the saddest widows are those who moved with a retired husband to some retirement "Shangri-la." Before they had a chance to make friends even as a couple, the husband died and left the woman a stranger in a strange environment.

Couples who may have been their friends don't want the widow around because she could be a threat to their happiness or well-being. This leaves the widow alone with other widows. In some retirement areas of Florida, for example, it's not uncommon to see widows dining, dancing, and socializing together. Some make the adjustment, however. Said one widow: "You know, some women think that only a man can take them to the movies or dinner. It took a while to get used to the idea of going alone or with another woman friend. But it works, and suddenly you find you're not limited because there are no men in the picture. You can set your own living pattern."

What about remarriage? Contrary to popular belief, most widows don't remarry. They cherish old memories or are afraid of having to nursemaid another ailing husband. One widow said: "I have no intention of remarrying, although I am normal with a fair share of sexual appetite. But I don't want a man to possess me body and soul."

What about the man who's a bachelor, divorced, or a widower? One man told me: "It's easy to have lady friends if you have your health and a little money. You buy a nice bottle of wine or a cake, and the lady fixes a dinner and a pleasant evening. Usually you can spend the night."

Most older men aren't interested in marrying again. One old-timer told me of an elderly man who liked companionship and frequently took lady acquaintances to dinner. Then one of his dining companions started to get serious. Finally she blurted: "Don't you think we should get married?" The courtly gent was equal to the occasion: "Yes," he replied, "but who would have us?"

Some Arrangements Are Better Than Some Marriages

Many singles would rather not live alone, but many have found that social security laws discriminate against widows or divorcées, or that children object—usually because they fear they'll lose an inheritance.

A former tax accountant said that when his wife died he wanted to marry a widow with five children, but his own children raised such a fuss that he threw in the sponge. So many older singles make "arrangements" without benefit of clergy or the Internal Revenue Service.

Statistics show that in the past ten years the number of unmarried couples living together increased by 820 percent! Of these, 72,200 couples are between the ages of twenty-five and sixty-four, and 18,200 couples are sixty-five and over. But the U.S. Census Bureau thinks the number is much higher, because couples who report themselves as living in a common-law marriage are listed as married.

"I think an 'arrangement' is a great idea, said one sixty-nine-year-old widow. I don't see why a woman has to give up her name, change her driver's license, credit cards, and everything."

But to quiet children, gossip, and their consciences, many couples maintain separate addresses although spending as much time together as possible. One woman explained: "When my daughter comes for a visit, Frank moves out. I don't want her to know; she'd think she'd be cut out of my will."

Another widow said: "I'm considering moving into the home of a slightly older widower and not marrying him. We both have a reasonable income, but mine comes almost entirely from my husband's will, which provides that if I remarry, the money goes to our children. If I don't remarry, I lose nothing. So why not be sensible?"

Widowers feel the same. A retired salesman met a schoolteacher several years from retirement; they decided to live together but not get married, because marriage would harm the teacher's pension rights. So life is a continuing "honeymoon" for this couple—regardless of status.

Cohabitation has advantages for the unmarried elderly. It provides husband-wife roles, a home, companionship, and—if desired—sex. Even if money isn't the main problem, the little extra money they may have by remaining single can make the difference between sitting at home or going out to dinner or to a show.

However, living together may *not* always be as enjoyable as a picnic. Don Harvey, director of the Family Services Center in Boston, said he counseled fifty unwed couples last year. "After the first couple of interviews, I can't tell who's married and who's living together. The dynamics and problems of the relationship are the same."

And the Rev. Dr. Benton Gaskell, minister of the Pilgrim United Church in Pomona, California, told of a couple who came to him for help: "They were in their seventies and living together clandestinely because they couldn't afford to marry, since they would lose pension income. They said they felt 'faithless' to their late spouses, never knew what to tell their children or friends, and were in spiritual distress over their predicament. They asked me to ease their guilt by solemnizing their union in the sight of God."

Dr. Stanley R. Dean, who has investigated many such arrangements, said: "My initial presumption had been that defiance of the law indicated neurotic traits and character defects, but further investigation revealed the surprising fact that most of those who circumvented the law were relatively stable, had adopted a good philosophical attitude, rationalized their guilt sufficiently well to maintain ego integrity, and were able to make a reasonably satisfactory psychological adjustment.

"The prevailing attitude seemed to be that the law was being bent rather than broken . . . no matter how tight things got, most of them put away a little money so it could be used when the masquerade was over—so they could be buried as they tried to live—decently."

Foster Homes, Communes, and Group Marriages

In many areas, people with large homes and empty rooms are turning them into "foster homes" for older adults. Although most homes have a lone proprietor or couple and only one or two older persons in residence, larger families with children have "adopted" four or more older people. The foster-home program (usually managed by the Human Resources Agency in a city) provides companionship, comfort, and safety for lonely elderly people.

Some older people are forming communes. In Winter Park, Florida, fifty-eight seniors—ranging in age from seventy to ninety-five—have been living as families along with a middle-aged couple who manage each of four homes.

The residents live their lives as they wish and do as much or as little work as they like. "We're all accomplished loafers, and we know how to enjoy our loafing," said one eighty-five-year-old resident. They read, play games, take trips, and help around the house when they feel like it. They pay the manager and his family to do most of the work.

Depending upon their financial status, members contribute from $275 to $300 a month for room and board. The residents must be ambulatory, and must provide a power of attorney to a person of their choice in case they become incapacitated.

The arrangement has worked out so well that a group of Winter Park citizens formed Share-a-Home of America, Inc., to collect money to set up homes in other communities.

In his book *Future Shock*, Alvin Toffler calls geriatric communes the "wave of the future." In communes, marital ties may be strictly observed or they may be disregarded. Either way, communes offer alternatives to single persons seeking companionship and even sex.

Dr. David L. Bradford, a Stanford University professor who has studied the subject, says that communes or households develop relationships more like brother and sister. As people become defined as a family, incest taboos develop. Benjamin Zablocki, a sociology professor at Columbia University, has said that only about 10 percent of commune members engaged in group sex activities.

Dr. Frieda Porat, author of *Changing Your Life Style,* says that for communes to last for more than a year and to win loyalty from members, they must begin with or soon develop a general purpose for being together. She says: "All advantages of communal living can be summarized in the general plan which provides as many options as possible for—self-knowledge, meaningful relationships, use of time, learning and growing."

Many thoughtful sociologists and gerontologists have suggested polygamy as a possible solution to financial and sexual security in the later years. During the period when the Mormons practiced polygamy, it solved the problem of excess women with minimum difficulty among the plural wives. The church supported polygamy, and it was abandoned only when the church decreed that it should be, because of legal and social harrassment.

Cupid in Retirement Villages

Most retirement villages are now called "adult communities" and cater to people in "their late forties and older." Probably the average is closer to sixty, with most residents being retired or semiretired couples.

Most adult communities offer scores of clubs, ranging from bridge and pinochle groups to community-service organizations. Activities structure the residents' lives, giving them a place to be at a certain time.

Most activities are geared to couples, as about 80 percent of the residents are married. But as the couples grow older, chances increase that the wives will become widows. Then they may be obliged to move into a "life-care residence" or a retirement home, where the average age may be in the seventies or eighties and where only about 20 percent of the residents are married.

Social life in life-care or retirement residences is more private, offering organized activities—bridge, an occasional travel movie, bingo once a month—and selective friendships to protect each other from bores and hangers-on. The residents are usually similar enough in age and social background so that they can wink at the occasional bachelor who might sneak a lady into his room.

Senior centers also offer many opportunties for romance. I've visited several where couples held hands in the TV room, and ardent swains of seventy wooed fair ladies of sixty. The competition sometimes becomes fierce, with jealous couples sending scorching glances across the room, and women growing possessive about their "boy-friends."

The Not-So-Happy Plight in Nursing Homes

Men and women in nursing homes are probably the most sexually deprived. There's little chance for privacy, and many homes "bedcheck" their patients. Dr. Mary S. Calderone tells of one home that forbade any unmarried man and woman to watch television together late in the evening.

Even married couples may be separated or allowed to mix only under supervision. One older woman said that when she suggested that the home's director put at least a three-quarter bed in her husband's room, the man looked at her as though she were some sort of "sex monster."

Jacob Reingold, executive director of the Hebrew Home for the Aged in the Bronx, New York, tells of the nurse who came running to him to report that an elderly couple were making love in the woman's room. "What should I do?" the nurse asked frantically. Answered Mr. Reingold: "Tiptoe so you don't disturb them."

Mr. Reingold adds that privacy is important to older people, because they separate what's right in public from what's right in private. Whereas an older woman might reject a man in public, she might accept him in private.

The American Association of Homes for the Aging is drawing

up a "Patient's Bill of Rights," which includes privacy for patients. And some homes for the aging have rooms where couples can meet privately—for talk, tea, or thee.

However, oldsters conflict with other residents. "My problems are with the ninety-year-old prudes," said the administrator of a Manhattan nursing center. "When an old man tries to climb into bed with another woman, it's usually the woman in the *other* bed who complains."

Future Shock or Future Sex?

In *Future Shock*, Alvin Toffler makes interesting speculations about the future of relationships of older people. He predicts these possibilities:

1. *Postponing the raising of children until after retirement.* Toffler says that men and women today are often torn between a commitment to a career and a commitment to raising children. Why not, then, buy embryos after your work career is over, then raise the children when you have more time to commit to them?

2. *Serial marriage.* Toffler suggests a trial marriage in youth, a second marriage in the early twenties when couples may formalize their relationship, and a third marriage that might stretch from the late thirties until one of the partners dies.

He says this last marriage may be the only "real" marriage, during which two mature people, with well-matched temperaments, will form a more permanent relationship. Even this marriage may suffer from "retirement shock," but it may be cemented by the postretirement family or by a new set of habits, interests, and activities. In these relationships, chronological age won't be as important as the psychological stage of life!

September Song May Be Sweeter Than May Wine

The Mexicans say that every man should marry three times: an older woman when he's young, so that he can learn the art of love . . . a woman his own age when he's middle-aged, so that he can practice what he's learned . . . a young girl when he's old, so that he can teach her.

The same philosophy applies to women. Studies of female sexuality and investigations into the sex lives of older people show that an older lover can do more for a young woman than pay her bills. As one twenty-six-year-old divorcée said: "I find that I much prefer middle-aged men to the younger ones. Young men are too frantic about sex. They go wild over it and seem to want sex only for its own sake. I get tired of that. When I wake up in the morning after that kind of encounter, I have a feeling of nothingness. A middle-aged man is *much* more concerned about the woman. He wants to both give and receive tenderness. He wants to be sure that nobody gets hurt; the *person* is important, not just sex. To the older man, the relationship with the woman comes first and the sexual act emerges from that. They show much more emotion—at least the kind of emotion that I like and can respond to. The older man demonstrates an air of protectiveness and concern for a girl, which is just not there with most younger men. Older men's behavior is geared toward my needs, but younger men are primarily concerned with their own needs."

Many young women like the overture better than the performance. Older men can arouse younger women with seductive words and subtle caresses—prolonging sex and not hurrying to orgasm. Men like Victor Hugo, Charles Chaplin, Pablo Picasso, and Pablo Casals prove that older men make excellent lovers for younger women.

Older women also make prime lovers for younger men. Dr. Eleanore B. Luckey, counselor and head of the Family Relations Department of the University of Connecticut, says, "There seems to be a growing trend for the mature woman to marry or to form an emotional liaison with a man considerably younger than herself."

In taking a younger lover, a woman subconsciously relives her youth and feels sexually appealing again. Doris Duke, Dinah Shore, Leslie Caron, Ruth Gordon have taken younger mates or lovers. The older woman who is sexually mature may form a perfect match with a younger man who is also sexually mature (at a much younger age). Said one twenty-eight-year-old lawyer who habitually dates older women: "I find older women more interesting, and they enjoy sex more than young girls. They're safe, don't want to get married, and make few demands. Also, they're more understanding than young girls, more willing to listen to your problems."

The older women also find fulfillment. One forty-five-year-old divorcée has had several affairs with men fifteen to twenty years younger because: "Some men my age are over the hill. For over twenty years I was a faithful wife with a husband who bored me in bed. But now that I'm a free agent again, I select sexual partners who can keep up with me." Older-women, younger-men relationships are increasingly common in Europe, especially in Britain, Sweden, and West Germany. In West Germany alone, of 450,000 marriages in 1973, 70,000 were between an older wife and a younger husband.

Dr. Calderone says: "I would look forward to open opportunity especially for women over 50 whose children may be grown or who might wish to change life-style, jobs, careers . . . I would look for the results of this kind of responsible freedom to be in terms of warmth, companionship, and emotional fulfillment for all men and women . . . "

Dr. Calderone also projects that men and women will be increasingly similar as to expectations, standards, and frequency of sexual behavior.

The Fires of Autumn Burn More Cozily Than Those of Spring

Sexuality in the middle and later years means more than physical sex . . . more than engaging in frenzied sexual encounters. For some it may express itself in the need for continued closeness, affection, and intimacy.

Whatever the expression of sexuality, society as well as ourselves should recognize the *normality of sex* in the middle and later years and our right to express it fully without feeling guilty.

Just as "too old for sex" is outmoded, so must all of us change our attitudes toward all aspects of sexuality in later years—the emotional as well as physical. Doctors, sociologists, psychologists must realize that negative attitudes on their part damage sexual expression on our part, and persons who build or administer housing for the elderly must take our sexual needs into account in their arrangements and treatments.

Unfortunately, cultural convention hasn't kept pace with social reality. Society has yet to recognize that the "code-book" on how we're expected to live is full of dictates for approved conduct during childbearing years, but none for the middle or later years. Thus, it's up to you and me to find the way for ourselves and for others to follow.

Although physical sex can bring us closer together, without *love* it can't bridge the emotional gap. Sexual *happiness* stems from emotional love—not sexual techniques. If a physically inhibited person becomes capable of loving, he/she will solve the sexual problems. If not, no amount of sexual technique will help.

Many authorities believe that our enjoyment will be increased when our present sexual ideals are replaced by ideals of affection, emotional expression, and warm human relationships. They say that companionship has emerged as the most valued aspect of human relationships today.

Dr. Martin Berezin, associate clinical professor at Harvard Medical School, believes that most sexual studies of later years put too much stress on physical activity. He says: "...none of these studies refers to something else, and that is love...tenderness... closeness. After all, a sex relationship is simply one kind of measure of how people are getting along with one another."

However, sexuality in the middle and later years exists in one form or another—from cuddling to copulating—in all studied individuals. For many, sexuality in middle and later years expresses itself in a *continuing interest* in physical and emotional sex, in the desire to make living a romantic adventure. The relationship between man and woman often depends upon their faith in and knowledge of themselves and each other. Loving is giving—sexually and emotionally. And the ability to love as an act of giving can be the highest expression of potency, raising the *art* of loving above the *act* of loving.

This depends upon the character of the person and the extent (depth) of his masculinity or her femininity. At any age a woman can express her femininity in her graceful way of walking, her stylish mode of dressing, her soft way of talking. At any age a man can show his masculinity through his gallant gestures, his concern for his partner, and his appearance. At any age, any of us can interchange "charm" with "sex appeal."

Once assured of our own masculinity or femininity, we can reach out to a partner. This requires not only knowledge—but effort. Plato said: "For love is the desire of the whole, and the pursuit of the whole is called love." Loving is living, and just as a rose must bloom to fulfill its living, so must human love blossom to fulfill living.

While sex affirms tenderness and togetherness, so can tenderness and affection affirm a relationship. A mutual exchange of affection—in whatever form—renews the faithful pact.

True love is an activity—a sharing and caring—between two people. Mature love is freely given; it's an action—something you *make* happen. If you will it to happen, you can will to love forever.

In this book I've tried to explore truths and explode myths of sexuality in the middle and later years. I've given you authoritative advice, personal experiences, and practical information to help you improve your sexuality.

Whatever you do, it doesn't matter—if you don't mind. By expressing your sexuality, you'll kindle a warm glow in yourself and in your partner. And however you live or love, you'll find that the Fires of Autumn are just as warm as—and a lot more comforting than—the Fires of Spring.